Receptive Ecumenism

Edited by Vicky Balabanski
and
Geraldine Hawkes

A Forum for Theology in the World
Volume 5, Issue 2, 2018

A Forum for a Theology in the World is an academic refereed journal aimed at engaging with issues in the contemporary world, a world which is pluralist and eucumenical in nature. The journal reflects this pluralism and ecumenism. Each edition is theme specific and has its own editor responsible for the production. The journal aims to elicit and encourage dialogue on topics and issues in contemporary society and within a variety of religious traditions. The Editor in Chief welcomes submissions of manuscripts, collections of articles, for review from individuals or institutions, which may be from seminars or conferences or written specifically for the journal. An internal peer review is expected before submitting the manuscript. It is the expectation of the publisher that, once a manuscript has been accepted for publication, it will be submitted according to the house style to be found at the back of this volume. All submissions to the Editor in Chief are to be sent to: hdregan@atf.org.au.

Each edition is available as a journal subscription, or as a book in print, pdf or epub, through the ATF Press web site — www.atfpress.com. Journal subscriptions are also available through EBSCO and other library suppliers.

Editor in Chief
Hilary Regan, ATF Press

A Forum for Theology in the World is published by ATF Theology and imprint of ATF (Australia) Ltd
(ABN 90 116 359 963) and
is published twice or three times a year.
ISSN 1329-6264

ATF Press
PO Box 504
Hindmarsh SA 5007
Australia
www.atfpress.com

Subscription Rates 2018

Print	On-Line	Print and On-line
Aust $65 Individuals	Aus $55 individuals	Aus $75 individuals
Aus $90 Institutions	Aus $80 individuals	Aus $100 instiutions

ISBN: 978-1-925643-91-6 (paperback)
        978-1-925643-92-3 (hardback)
        978-1-925643-93-0 (epub)
        978-1-925643-94-7 (pdf)

Receptive Ecumenism

Listening, Learning and Loving in the Way of Christ

Edited by Vicky Balabanski
and
Geraldine Hawkes

Adelaide
2018

Table of Contents

Introduction

Vicky Balabanski and Geraldine Hawkes

Your eye is the lamp of your body. If your eye is healthy, your whole body is full of light; but if it is not healthy, your body is full of darkness. Therefore consider whether the light in you is not darkness. If then your whole body is full of light, with no part of it in darkness, it will be as full of light as when a lamp gives you light with its rays. Luke 11:34–6 (NRSV)

Receptive Ecumenism—listening, learning and loving in the Way of Christ is a response to the growing recognition of Receptive Ecumenism as a concept and process that has the potential to assist renewal and reform of the whole Church, both from within denominations as well as across the Church universal.

Since 2006, when Professor Paul Murray of the University of Durham organised and hosted the first Receptive Ecumenism conference, there have been three further international conferences on Receptive Ecumenism. The feasibility of a fifth is currently being explored. During these years, Receptive Ecumenism has caught the imagination of a wide range of people from various churches. A diverse and rich discourse has resulted, with a variety of papers and practical projects, in ways that are dynamic, creative and responsive to whatever part of the church the participants find themselves in, and a new sense of hope and possibility about being church has flowed.

However, despite such activity and the significant influence that Receptive Ecumenism is having, there is relatively little published on it so far. This volume is a contribution to filling this gap, inspired by the most recent International Conference, held in Canberra, Australia in November 2017.

It is helpful at this point also to reflect on the current shape or 'appearance' of ecumenical work so far, and how we might recognise Receptive Ecumenism.

There has been ecumenical co-operation and dialogue across churches in various arenas for many years. These have helped build respectful relationships and understanding among us, and generally serve our world well. However, involvement seems to be limited to the interested few, rather than to the greater whole. Various parts of the life and mission of each tradition seem untouched, understandably perhaps, by the fruitfulness of the ecumenical movement; energy for ecumenism has dissipated a little, and in some arenas conflicting sets of values permeate our attitudes, behaviour and language with and towards one another.

Over the years churches have created parishes, boards, committees, councils, synods, agencies, universities, hospitals and more, generally with a sound theological basis. However, as they evolve and are re-shaped, they can succumb to other demands and may unintentionally lose the distinctive light of the Gospel.

While learning about and co-operating with one another remains important, alongside creating structures and processes for sharing, transmitting and living faith, there is a need also to be attentive to those parts of the interior ecclesial life of one's own church that may not fully reflect the Way of Christ. The health of our ecclesial 'eyes', to use the biblical metaphor, is not what it could be, and the light of Christ does not radiate throughout the body as fully as it might.

Receptive Ecumenism encourages awareness of one's own institutional weaknesses and fragilities, and offers an approach for dealing with any part of Church life that needs reconciling. This is the very place where Receptive Ecumenism may enter.

Receptive Ecumenism does not ask us to focus on another church's wounds, weaknesses or vulnerabilities, nor to be telling them about where we think they are wrong and need to be healed. Rather, it is about a healthy recognition of one's own need for healing, through discerning from time to time any place within our structures, systems, practices and processes that may be oppressing, obscuring, diminishing or even extinguishing the light of Christ, or blocking people from being drawn closer into Christ and towards one another.

Receptive Ecumenism is seemingly simple. It invites us to ask not *'What do we have to tell, or learn about, the other?'*, but rather *'What do we need to learn from the other?'*

The complexity emerges as people begin the profound turn-around that a Receptive Ecumenical approach requires, if people are to grow in being truly able to recognise the need within one's own tradition, and to seek out another, in the hope of discovering, discerning and receiving with integrity the 'gift' of the other.

Following years of activity together, of describing ourselves to the other, and of feeling certain and sure about our own churches, Receptive Ecumenism draws us into a new disposition, and a new way of speaking and relating with one another.

Some current bi/multi-lateral dialogues or actions make use of words like dialogue, debate, mutual confidence, discussions, building of trust and the reduction of fear, and these are important concepts in ecumenism. However, Receptive Ecumenism does not require us to be in dialogue, debate, or even discussion. It does not need us to wait for the other, nor is it dependent on the other being concerned in any way about the need for their own healing or learning. The other does not even need to be remotely interested in ecumenism.

Receptive Ecumenism is a self-reflective posture before it is one of interrogating the other. It is a shift from dialogue and telling, to deep self-examination and listening. It includes discernment and learning, without judgement of, from or by the other, or expecting anything in return. It is about a culture of hospitality, of thinking and acting with love and humility; of being open to recognising our own ecclesial imperfections; of learning to recognise the other as gift; and of being open to receiving with integrity the wisdom and gift of the other in the same way as God receives them.

The hope is, therefore, that this publication will appeal to and assist not only the interested ecumenist or academic, but any individual or church body with a yearning for renewal and reform, with integrity, and all who have responsibility within any setting of Church.

The papers offer a wide-ranging understanding of Receptive Ecumenism, descriptions of the values undergirding it, as well as frameworks, methods and applications of Receptive Ecumenism to encourage, inspire and assist our flourishing together in the Way of Christ, in, with and for the world.

While there remain aspects and practices to be more deeply explored and understood, especially around what ecclesial discernment and reception with integrity look like, the hope is that each paper will inspire us / people to contribute to further discoveries.

Additionally, there is the hope that this publication will be a means of connecting people interested in this rapidly growing movement, to ignite the imagination of those who are curious, and to nurture us all theologically, spiritually and practically, not as separated Christians, but as a community of disciples, so that the body may fully radiate the light of Christ.

Paul Murray, the initiator of Receptive Ecumenism, offers two important, invitational and insightful reflections to open and close this volume—the Foreword and the Afterword. They form essential reading and deep consideration before and following the reading of, and acting on, this collection of essays.

The volume continues with three contributions that invite an engagement with Receptive Ecumenism through imagination and affect as well as through reason and intellect. By opening the volume in this way, we acknowledge that to practise ecumenism *receptively* requires not only an appropriate conceptual framework and rigorous intellectual discussion, but also an openness to engage with people who differ from ourselves with a 'gaze of love'. Such a gaze involves a degree of vulnerability to the other and necessarily involves the heart as well as the mind. By imaginatively entering into the biblical narrative and attending to what it has to say both to and about us, we allow ourselves to be formed according to the image of Christ. Such a formative process involves the whole person. Receptive Ecumenism thus cultivates receptivity not only towards the other, but also towards the Holy Spirit's guidance through the biblical narrative.

The first contribution is a guided meditation by Geraldine Hawkes. It invites the reader to enter into a self-reflective engagement with a striking visual text portraying the encounter between Jesus and the woman of Samaria. The movement of Receptive Ecumenism is mirrored in this meditation, and it can be used to accompany the reading of the essays that follow.

There follow two Bible studies by Vicky Balabanski. The first of these, with a focus on Colossians 3:11–17, explores how clothing ourselves with Christ means finding our identity not in the outward markers by which we differentiate ourselves from one another, but by expanding our gaze to perceive that 'Christ is all and in all' (Col 3:11). The second Bible study on Romans 8:18–30 places ecumenism in an eschatological context; this invites us to look beyond our own boundaries and glimpse the big picture of the *missio Dei*. The big picture shows that God's concern is not only for humanity, but for all creation, which eagerly longs for the children of God to be revealed— a truly ecumenical revelation of a restored relationship between God, creation and humanity. Our unity is shaped by the eschatological future to which God is calling us.

The essays that follow are grouped according to their respective emphases on one of the three aspects of the Way of Christ named in the title of the volume: listening, learning and loving. Each of these is characteristic of Receptive Ecumenism and describes a core aspect of its approach to ecumenical engagement. How do we listen and discern what may be a gift of God? How can we learn from the other with integrity? In what ways does the approach of Receptive Ecumenism lead to loving that reflects the love of God?

Denis Edwards opens the section on 'Listening'. In dialogue with an insight of Karl Rahner on the experience of the Spirit of God, he explores the spiritual logic of Christian decision-making. Edwards sets out the way the experience of grace, which is indeed the experience of the Spirit, functions as a kind of first principle in the logic of this process, and how it leads over time towards the deepest sense of self. Edwards argues that there is a parallel at the level of Church to what Rahner proposes at the level of the individual, and tests this proposal in relation to the institutional charism of synodality, offered to the Roman Catholic Church by, among others, the Anglican, Lutheran and Orthodox churches.

In the next essay, Karen Petersen Finch takes up the issue of ecumenical discernment, this time in dialogue with Jesuit theologian and philosopher Bernard Lonergan, who argued that discernment includes an element of decision. Finch sets out Lonergan's cognitional theory in four cognitive 'operations': experience, understanding, judgment and decision, and draws out the significance of these for ecumenical discernment. She argues that the method we adopt is important in this process, and it assists as we move towards conversion–not only religious, but intellectual and moral.

The essay by Elizabeth Welch focusses on the Holy Spirit and communion. Welch sets out some key aspects of the work of the Spirit in enabling various levels of communion: first the transformative role of the Holy Spirit in bringing about communion (understood as the relationality that is possible with God); second, the Spirit drawing God's people into a communion that is embodied in prayer and worship, and third, the eschatological dimension of the work of the Spirit in bringing about communion. She concludes with a consideration of the International Reformed Anglican Dialogue as a dialogue between and about communion.

The second section of this collection, with a focus on 'Learning', opens with Antonia Pizzey's essay, 'Receptive Ecumenical Learning: A Constructive Way of Approaching Ecclesial Identity and Renewal'. She sets out how Receptive Ecumenism, while affirming the continued importance of both practical and theological ecumenism, directs our attention beyond learning about each other (theological ecumenism) and simply co-operating with each other (practical ecumenism) to focus on learning *from* each other (Receptive Ecumenism). She explores one of the most significant challenges facing ecclesial learning and church renewal today, namely that of ecclesial identity, and argues that Receptive Ecumenism offers a helpful strategy when grappling with issues surrounding ecclesial identity and learning.

Doru Costache, as an Eastern Orthodox scholar in the diaspora, reflects on the benefits of a receptive ecumenical approach in his essay 'Contemporary Orthodox Diaspora: Learning from a Lutheran–Roman Catholic Document'. With a focus on the Lutheran–Roman Catholic ecumenical document *The Ministry of Oversight* (2007), Costache considers what the Eastern Orthodox diaspora could learn from its approach and findings. He gives insight into the specific challenges faced by Australian Orthodoxy, including the pressure to define themselves as migrant communities, which leads to Eastern Orthodox jurisdictions coexisting within one place but not sharing in each other's life. He advocates the need to learn what it means to listen to one another, in order to contextualise each's message, and be capable of recognising shared values beyond cultural differences.

The learning continues with Geraldine Hawkes offering a description of three processes to assist in nurturing a receptive disposition and a practical engagement with Receptive Ecumenism.

John Littleton's essay explores linking the approach of Receptive Ecumenism with learning community strategies to enhance ecumenical learning within and between learning communities. He gives consideration to Ecumenical Learning, as defined by the World Council of Churches, and particularly Simon Oxley's concept that ecumenical education helps churches become learning communities rather than domesticating communities, having a broad or multiple perspectives rather than a single, narrow view of their faith and the world. Littleton then describes parishes which function as learning communities when holistic, collaborative and theologically reflective processes are intentionally practised. He gives some examples of how receptive ecumenism is being practised in his own context of South Australia.

Sweden is the context for the final essay in this section. Sara Gehlin sets out the pedagogical process which Receptive Ecumenism inspired in the four 'church families' recognised by the Christian Council of Sweden: the Orthodox, Catholic, Lutheran, and Free Church families. The overarching shape of the pedagogical process was that of a Pilgrimage, and Gehlin sets this out under the key components of *place and movement, theme, structure, dynamics, challenges, time-frames*, and *goals*. Gehlin's reflection on the two-year process offers insight into the generative nature of the process, which brought about deeper knowledge of the ways in which mission is lived and understood within the four church families, mutual enrichment between traditions and interpersonal trust and ecumenical friendship.

The final section of the collection, under the heading of 'Loving', offers three essays that engage at depth with the approach of Receptive Ecumenism. Gabrielle Thomas focusses on the application of hospitality, which has been named in various places as a vital virtue in the practice of Receptive Ecumenism. She describes the steps taken by a group of women in the UK and the role of hospitality in creating safe spaces for learning and for gifts to be received. In making the link between the action of the women and Christ's hospitality, Gabrielle challenges the churches in their own hospitality towards women and the need to ensure the full reception of the gifts that women have to share. Gregory Ryan's essay challenges us to consider its theological and hermeneutical roots in order to avoid superficial appropriations of it. He sets out Paul Murray's overall methodological strategy, of which Receptive Ecumenism is one outworking, under the heading of 'Dynamic integrity'.

Ryan points out that part of the distinctiveness of Receptive Ecumenism is that, at least initially, it is oriented not towards direct consensus *between* traditions, but rather towards refreshing, expanding healing *within* a tradition through learning from the other. He brings this into fruitful conversation with reception hermeneutics, the work of Ormond Rush, showing that there is a structural and dynamic resonance between Murray's approach and Rush's hermeneutics which offers a rich field of exploration.

The final essay in the collection is by Callan Slipper, who sees a profound parallel between the cruciform love of Christ and the spiritual logic of Receptive Ecumenism. Drawing on ancient and contemporary trinitarian theology, he sets out the pattern of relationship in both as love which adopts a truly listening, comprehending and attentive stance. Slipper goes on to explore the way Receptive Ecumenism, when practised according to the full meaning of its theological depth, is an eschatological event. He concludes with a reflection on the major Receptive Ecumenism project in the North East of England, and emphasises the need for taking the eschatological dimension of such projects seriously. It is this horizon which shows that there is a possibility of experiencing the ultimate unity even before that unity is fully reached. He concludes that the final end is effective in the present means.

We express our gratitude to Peter Balabanski for his constant and expert attention to the written word and syntax, and to those at ATF Press for their willingness to respond quickly and generously in making this volume possible and for their assiduous work in bringing this to fruition.

We began this introduction with an acknowledgement of the fact that there has been relatively little published to date on Receptive Ecumenism. We offer this volume as a contribution to redressing this need, trusting that the Way of Christ will be made more accessible by it, and that we may join one another in this path towards our shared future.

A Forum for Theology in the World Vol 5 No 2/2018

Foreword
Receptive Ecumenism as a Leaning-in to the Spirit of Loving Transformation

Paul D Murray

It is a great pleasure and honour to offer both a Foreword and an Afterword to this diverse volume which explores and celebrates Receptive Ecumenism.

Geraldine Hawkes' profound 'Meditation on the Water of Life', inspired by reflection on the beautiful sculpture from Chester Cathedral featured on the front cover, and Vicky Balabanski's highly apposite biblical reflections form a powerful entry point. Together with Antonia Pizzey's and Callan Slipper's contributions, these pieces variously serve to take us deeply into the spirit and soul of Receptive Ecumenism.

In turn, the contributions of Sara Gehlin, John Littleton, Doru Costache, and Gabrielle Thomas each extend this spiritual practice of—in the words of the editors—*listening, learning, and loving in the way of Christ* to fresh contexts: that of the ecumenical pilgrimages promoted by the Swedish Mission Council (Gehlin); that of the churches as intentional learning communities (Littleton); that of possible honest diasporal Orthodox self-recognition and receptive learning relative to the fruits of Lutheran-Catholic dialogue (Costache); and in relation to what can be learned of the ways of mutual hospitality from women's ecclesial experiences in the churches in the United Kingdom (Thomas). For her own part, Karen Petersen Finch provides a very clear presentation of Bernard Lonergan's approach to theological rationality and method, and reflects on its relevance for ecclesial decision-making in a way that might open some ground for Lonergan scholars to explore what connections can be made with Receptive Ecumenism.[1]

---

1. Of relevance here is Catherine E Clifford, 'Lonergan's Contribution to Ecumenism', in *Theological Studies*, 63 (2002): 521–38.

With all of this, and as I explore further in the Afterword, Elizabeth Welch is correct to point to pneumatology as being key to the
thought and practice of Receptive Ecumenism. As, however, this
should also hopefully suggest, if there is a spiritual soul and instinct at
work in the practice of Receptive Ecumenism—what St Bonaventure
and the Franciscan tradition would refer to as *affectus*[2]—it is important to keep clearly in mind that this is a spiritual practice and mode
of understanding which needs to be explicitly theologically inflected,
reflected, shaped, and scrutinised throughout by the power of intellect (*intellectus*) and reason (*ratio*).[3] Working in inextricable associa-

---

2. For example, St Bonaventure, *1 Sent.* proe., q.3, resp, in *Opera Theologica Selecta*
    (Firenze: Quaracchi, 1934), p. 11; also St Bonaventure, *Works of St Bonaventure,
    Vol. IX. Breviloquium*, translated by Dominic Monti, OFM (New York: Franciscan
    Institute Publications, 2005), 17; also St Bonaventure, Collation 2, n.32, in
    Collations on the Six Days, translated by Jose De Vinck (Paterson, NJ: St Anthony
    Guild Press, 1970), 39; and St Bonaventure, qq.6-7, in *Works of St. Bonaventure,
    Volume IV. Disputed Questions on the Knowledge of Christ*, translated by Zachary
    Hayes, OFM (New York: Franciscan Institute Publications, 2005), 161–194. I am
    grateful to William Crozier for identifying these and all other Bonaventurian
    references here; as too, more generally, for conversations on the theology of St
    Bonaventure stretching over some years now.
3. Something of a parallel again pertains with St Bonaventure, for whom the assent
    of love necessarily entails the use of reason: 'But when faith does not assent
    because of reason, but because of love for Him to whom it assents, it desires to
    have reasons (*desiderat habere rationem*). And when this happens it does not
    empty human reason (*ratio humana*) of its merits; instead, it serves to augment
    consolation.' St Bonaventure, *1 Sent.*, proe., q.2, ad.6, in *Opera Theologica Selecta*,
    as translated by William Crozier (Firenze: Quaracchi, 1934), 10. For his own
    part and operating within the Thomistic tradition, Joseph Pieper distinguishes
    between 'the understanding as *ratio* and the understanding as *intellectus*' in a
    way which might initially sound as though it helpfully maps onto this Franciscan
    affectus/ratio-intellectus distinction. Pieper writes: '*Ratio* is the power of
    discursive, logical thought, of searching and of examination, of abstraction, of
    definition and drawing conclusions. *Intellectus*, on the other hand, is the name
    for the understanding in so far as it is the capacity of *simplex intuitus*, of that
    simple vision to which truth offers itself like a landscape to the eye.' Josef Pieper,
    Leisure, the Basis of Culture, translated by Alexander Dru with an Introduction
    by TS Eliot (London: Faber and Faber, 1952 [1948]), 33–4; also, 'The mode of
    discursive thought is accompanied and impregnated by an effortless awareness,
    the contemplative vision of the *intellectus* . . .' 34. Indeed, for present purposes—
    that is in the context of our discussing Receptive Ecumenism—it is particularly
    notable that Pieper refers to *intellectus* as 'not active but passive, or rather
    receptive, the activity of the soul in which it conceives that which it sees'. 34,

tion with the receptive spiritual soul of Receptive Ecumenism is a beating theological heart and intentional mind-set. Sure, without the former's close attentiveness to the in-*spiring* movement of the Spirit, the latter will tend towards being mere concept, dead letter, and frustrated strategy. Equally, however, without the latter, which involves due attention to the need for disciplined theological testing and strategising, the former will tend towards directionless desire and mere aspiration. Alternatively stated, this relates to the inextricable and necessary enfolding of the Pneumatic and the Christic, with the former as the movement and energy of God's being-in-act and the latter as its expressed form.

It is particularly good, then, to have included here the pieces by Denis Edwards, who demonstrates a clear grasp of the theological dynamics of Receptive Ecumenism in his various essays on the subject, and Gregory Ryan, who, with a deep appreciation for the theological infrastructure of Receptive Ecumenism, is in process of making a significant contribution to its substantive development and further dissemination in a way prefaced in his contribution here and shortly to come to full extended publication in its own right.

Gregory Ryan's reflections concern the hermeneutical process at work in Receptive Ecumenism and how this might be clarified and deepened by being brought into relationship with Ormond Rush's work on reception hermeneutics. As already alluded to, Vicky Balabanski and Geraldine Hawkes helpfully refer to this hermeneutical

---

emphasis added; also 'Our knowledge in fact includes an element of non-activity, of purely receptive vision . . . ', 35; and ' . . . in the same way his (*sic*) great, imperishable intuitions visit a man in his moments of leisure. It is in these silent and receptive moments that the soul of man is sometimes visited by an awareness of what holds the world together . . ', 54.. For such reasons the unwary reader might falsely assume: a) that *intellectus* in the Thomistic tradition maps onto *affectus* in the Franciscan tradition, with Bonaventure's less differentiated use of *intellectus* equating more specifically to the Thomistic *ratio*; and b) that in this way the supposed contrast between the priority of love in the Franciscan tradition and the priority of reason in the Thomistic tradition might be helpfully relativized. However, as Rik van Nieuwenhove carefully and clearly establishes, St Thomas' use of *intellectus* (compare 'insight') and *ratio* each pertain to distinct intellectual operations of the mind and not to the realm of intuition, love, or spiritual knowledge. See Rik van Nieuwenhove, 'Contemplation, Intellectus, and *Simplex Intuitus* in Aquinas: Recovering a Neoplatonic Theme', in *American Catholic Philosophical Quarterly*, 91/2 (2017): 199–225.

process with the three-fold movement of *listening, learning, and loving*. The various naming of three-fold movements and concerns has been a recurrent theme in writing on Receptive Ecumenism—indeed Gregory Ryan further extends this by drawing on Ormond Rush's own three-fold forms—and it is interesting to note the resonance that sounds between these various usages.

The *listening, learning, loving* of this volume correlates well with the three-fold *attending to what is, discerning what might be*, and *acting to realise the future* which I have elsewhere identified as describing the fundamental movements of human rationality and, indeed, of all true, beautiful, and good human engagement with reality.[4] There I also played upon these movements as having some resonance *both* with the always interrelated and mutually associated cardinal virtues of faith, hope, and charity—which are correctly understood as three facets of one God-initiated and God-sustained orientation of life—*and* with the inextricably interrelated form of our three-fold dependence on God's being-in-act as inexhaustible Source (Father), expressed Form/Logos (Son), and in-*spirating* Energy (Spirit). When theologically situated and configured in this manner, each of these fundamental movements of human engagement with reality is properly lived as a faith-held and hope-filled movement in love—and first and foremost not our love for God but God's love for us (see 1 Jn 4:10) which 'has been poured into our hearts through the Holy Spirit' (Rom 5:5) who *is* the 'spring' of 'living water' which has been promised us (Jn 4:10–14).

In turn, it was reflection upon these various three-fold movements—combined with a concern to bring praxis-oriented theology and properly systematic theology into closer correlation with each other—which lay behind my varying articulations of the task of theology as consisting in: i) critical-constructive analysis of the understanding and practice of faith and the questions, problems, difficulties, and possibilities which arise there (compare *attending in faith*); with a view to ii) identifying and scrutinising the viability of potential ways ahead through various modes of coherence-based testing (compare *discerning in hope*); and so iii) being able to enhance the quality of

---

4. See Paul D Murray, *Reason, Truth, and Theology in Pragmatist Perspective* (Leuven: Peeters, 2004).

the understanding, practice, and witness of faith (compare *acting in love*).[5]

This is systematic theology in interrogative-pragmatic mode, concerned to think through rigorously and systematically that which arises on the way of Christian faith and which even lies in its path as obstacle and obstruction. This includes but is by no means exclusively limited to the traditional systematic concern to give a coherent account of the 'hope that is in us' (1 Pet 3:15) in a manner fitting for the times and places in which we find ourselves. Indeed the full range of concerns arising within this interrogative-pragmatic understanding of the systematic theological task extends well beyond this traditional aspiration for systematic presentation, stretching to encompass the full extent of Christian faith. For my own part, for example, a wide-ranging commitment to transformative ecclesiology stands as one general manifestation of this pursuit of systematic theology in interrogative-pragmatic mode and, closely related to this, the thought and practice of Receptive Ecumenism stands as another. It is essential to keep this systematically pursued, interrogative-pragmatic dimension of Receptive Ecumenism clearly in view, together with the commitment to rigorous, multi-levelled coherence-based scrutiny and testing which it represents.[6]

---

5.   See Paul D Murray, 'Searching the Living Truth of the Church in Practice: On the Transformative Task of Systematic Ecclesiology', in *Modern Theology*, 30 (2014): 251–81. For the relevance here of praxis-oriented theology, see, for example, Ignacio Ellacuría, 'Theology as the Ideological Moment of Ecclesial Praxis' (1978), translated by Anna Bonta Moreland and Kevin F Burke, in *Essays on History, Liberation, and Salvation*, edited and introduction by Michael E Lee and commentary by Kevin F Burke (Maryknoll, NY: Orbis, 2013), 255–73, where on 257 we find: 'And even when one does not presume a practical end explicitly, it is clear that the theologian and his or her supposed academic work are configured by the desire to respond to certain challenges, even if the responses are quite distinct from the challenges.'

6.   To be explicit: there is a combined emphasis here *both* on the necessarily rigorous, critical, scrutinising function of theology—all in accordance with various levels of coherence-based consideration—*and* on the need for this to be understood as being clearly situated as a key moment *within* a far broader process of Christian engagement and understanding that is coextensive with, as I put it, 'the full extent of Christian faith'. There is two-fold resonance here: on the one hand with St Thomas' emphasis on the specific contribution of theological analysis to Christian life and wisdom being in the mode of a theoretical science, which proceeds through rational analysis and understanding; on the other hand

As the Introduction to this volume makes clear, Receptive Ecumenism definitely shares in the interrogative-pragmatic commitment to starting with felt problems and difficulties in the understanding and practice of faith. As such, its founding principle should not be confused with a somewhat vague openness to valuing the other and potentially supplementing the existing secure strengths of one's own tradition with whatever might also be gleaned from the other's tradition. Rather, Receptive Ecumenism is a much sharper matter of starting with honest, repentant recognition of one's own tradition's significant difficulty in some specific regard and, with this clearly in view, then turning with a sense of urgent need to examine what might be potentially helpful in another tradition in some equally specific regard; and all whilst also recognising that any such potential receptive learning will require rigorous testing and a certain transposition and adaptation from one tradition to the other. It is in this way that Receptive Ecumenism seeks to serve the renewal and reform of the whole church, *both from within* particular communities/traditions *and between them.*

In the varying ways in which this is expressed in the literature on Receptive Ecumenism, sometimes the emphasis falls more on the felt sense of need and incapacity in relation to some aspect of one's own tradition's structures, systems, practices, processes, and understanding, with the result that language of ecclesial repentance, conversion, and reform is to the fore. At other times the emphasis falls more on the sense of attracted desire for what is discovered in the other tradition, to the point of even describing Receptive Ecumenism as a process of 'falling in love' which is drawn by and held within the one movement

---

with St Bonaventure's—and the wider Franciscan—emphasis on the theological process, most broadly construed, as being a practical, or 'living', science with a distinctly experiential basis informed by Christian life. Indeed, the discerning reader will correctly hear here a call for St Thomas' emphasis on the properly theoretical moment of theological analysis to be more clearly situated within the Bonaventurian/Franciscan understanding of the start and end of the theological process being most fundamentally practical in orientation. Moreover, the presupposition at work here is that such a resituating accords better both with St Thomas' own existential orientation—as a friar of the Order of Preachers, for whom theology is in service of Christian life—and with his own acknowledgment that theology is indeed related to the need for wisdom in Christian living. Too much can be and has been made of the supposed distinction between the respective approaches of St Thomas and St Bonaventure in this specific regard.

of love that is the Holy Spirit. For example, in the 'Preface' to the first Receptive Ecumenism volume, I described the three-fold process of *attending*, *discerning*, and *acting* in terms of the imaginative *poetics* and *poiesis* of the 'dreaming of dreams', the *analytics* of testing and scrutinising, and the pragmatics of institutional realisation.[7]

This prompts the question as to how this somewhat upbeat emphasis on the 'dreaming of dreams' sits together with the apparently more sombre emphasis elsewhere on the need to start with honest and repentant recognition of one's own tradition's difficulties? Well they sit together as two facets of the one movement of grace. In the extraordinary of Christian existence it is entirely ordinary for repentant recognition of our dysfunction to be held in and met by ever-renewed assurance of the real possibility of healing, new life, and limitless, inexhaustible love 'pressed down' and 'running over' (Lk 6:38). The process of attending in the Spirit to the difficulties in our own tradition can break up the ground and awaken a sharpened sense of need in us which can prepare us for the recognition of attractive graced gift in the other. Equally, it might be the surprising force of desire for what we find attractive in the other which evokes in us a clearer sense of our own need and which enables us to look more clearly at our own lacks and difficulties. Even before we are fully conscious of it and able to reflect upon it, desire for something from without can be drawing and moving us in the depths of our affective lives;[8] before our becoming intentionally responsive in their regard, we are in the situation of being attracted by perceived goods and loves which resonate with hungers and senses of need and lack in us.[9] Such desire has the capacity to move us to take steps we would not otherwise take.

---

7. See Paul D Murray, 'Preface', in *Receptive Ecumenism and the Call to Catholic Learning: Exploring a Way for Contemporary Ecumenism*, edited by Paul D Murray (Oxford: Oxford University Press, 2008), ix–xv, xi–xv.

8. Significant again here is the way in which St Bonaventure writes of God's self-communication to the soul through the prompting of grace as eliciting a response of desiring, loving attention before it issues in speculative reflection, see St Bonaventure, 'Collation 1: An Introductory Treatment of Grace According to Its Origin, Use, and Fruit', in *Works of St Bonaventure, Vol. XIV. Collations on the Seven Gifts of the Holy Spirit*, translated by Zachary Hayes, OFM (New York: Franciscan Institute Publications, 2008), 27–44.

9. In Catholic tradition, the most fundamental 'good and love' that is other than us by nature (compare 'something from without') but which draws and moves us in the depths of our affective lives is first, finally, and constantly throughout

Either way, when the movement of attending in the Spirit to our own and the other's reality is lent wings and achieves take-off then we have need and desire conjoined: both repentant recognition and the dreaming of dreams. This is the holy erotics of Receptive Ecumenism, which has the capacity to move our imaginations, wills, determinations, and minds to find ways, with dynamic integrity, to overcome the obstacles which stand in the way of consummated full communion.

This appears to bring us full circle and to return us to the image of Receptive Ecumenism as an affair of the heart, a Spirit-led soul-journey of intuition and desire. It is for good reason that the literature on Receptive Ecumenism works with the image of Christian life as a "*leaning-in* to the Spirit", with the Spirit figured here as uncontrolled, uncontrollable, initiating-sustaining-transforming Pentecostal power into whom we can lean our full weight and who sets us on our feet, energising and impelling us into action.[10]

But where the heart leads, the head (*intellectus/ratio*) must follow and there do its crucial critical work of testing, scrutinising, and

---

the Spirit, the personal loving agency of God. In as much as this is so, we are touching here on the experiential, existential roots of the Thomistic theology of the concurrence of divine and human action, with the latter always situated within and made possible by the former. Something of this is suggested by the opening words of Micheal O'Siadhail's remarkable *Five Quintets*:

> Be with me, Madam Jazz, I urge you now,
> Riff in me so I can conjure how
> You breathe in us more than we dare allow.

Micheal O'Siadhail, *The Five Quintets* (Wako, TX: Baylor University Press, 2018), xxiii. The appropriate spiritual correlate to the theology of concurrence would be a constant prayer of 'O Holy Spirit, move my desire that I might the more desire your moving of me.' Equally, in as much as the effects of sin are such that we are always confused in our sensing, perceiving, and responding to this constant prevenient draw and sustaining act of the Spirit, then we touch here also on the experiential, existential roots of temptation—and this before even introducing the question as to whether other fallen agencies are also at work, as the tradition has clearly maintained, in the experience of temptation.

10. For the image of 'leaning-in to the Spirit', see, for example, Paul D Murray, 'St Paul and Ecumenism: Justification and All That', in *New Blackfriars* (March 2010): 142–70, 168–9. The primary reference at work here is to the experience of being able to lean one's entire body weight into a strong wind and feeling oneself supported. This images a form of dependency which far from infantilising us (contra Nietzsche) serves rather to set us on our feet and to impel us forward. Equally, the image of 'leaning-in' might be extended as a pneumatological metaphor in line with the experience of balancing and enabling a speeding yacht, with full wind in the sail, by leaning out and back into the wind.

discerning. For as St Ignatius of Loyola recognised in his rules for the discernment of spirits, and as alluded to above, affairs of the heart and the imagination can lead to illusion and difficulty as well as to life and freedom.[11] Desire and love might give us the energy to move but their promptings can also be confused and impractical. Receptive Ecumenism, as with the broader understanding of the theological task of which it is one expression, might represent a certain charismatic resituating and reenergising of ecumenical engagement and endeavour but it is one which far from displacing the formal theological aspect of ecumenism intends rather to put it back clearly in its proper place, as the critical-constructive faculty of diagnosing, re-imagining, and testing in the way of Christian life. Spirit and Word, the charismatic and the Christic, are inextricably conjoined and necessarily interrelated. The movement of attending to what is and dreaming dreams properly opens into the testing of what is really possible.

All readers will be indebted to Vicky Balabanski and Geraldine Hawkes for their work in assembling with ATF Press this collection of explorations in *listening*, *learning*, and *loving* in the way of Receptive Ecumenism, which is a way of following in the way of Christ by leaning-in to the Spirit of loving transformation. Geraldine Hawkes' core involvement in encouraging an Australian team to organise and host the Fourth Receptive Ecumenism International—the first such to be organised without any significant involvement of the Centre for Catholic Studies at Durham University—as too her co-editing of this volume, are further expressions of the crucial initiating and energising role which she and colleagues within the South Australian Council of Churches have played in promoting the Australian reception and development of Receptive Ecumenism.

---

11. See St Ignatius of Loyola, 'Rules for Discernment', *The Spiritual Exercises of Saint Ignatius of Loyola*, §§313-36, translated by Michal Ivens, SJ, with an Introduction by Gerard W Hughes, SJ, (Leominster: Gracewing, 2004), 94–101. For commentary, see Ivens, *Understanding the Spiritual Exercises* (Leominster: Gracewing, 1998), 205–37, I am grateful to Sr Avril O'Regan, RLR, for drawing my attention to this source; also Jules J Toner, SJ, *A Commentary on St Ignatius' Rules for the Discernment of Spirits: A Guide to the Principles and Practice* (St Louis, MI: The Institute of Jesuit Sources, 1982), I am grateful to Rev Lynn McChlery for drawing my attention to this source; and Michael J Buckley, 'Rules for the Discernment of Spirits', in *The Way*, 20 (Autumn 1973): 19–37, reprinted in *The Way of Ignatius Loyola: Contemporary Approaches to the Spiritual Exercises*, edited by Philip Sheldrake (London: SPCK, 1991), 219–37.

A Forum for Theology in the World Vol 5 No 2/2018

A Meditation on the Water of Life

Geraldine Hawkes

The image on the cover of this publication has been chosen for the way it conveys certain elements of Receptive Ecumenism.

It shows a sculpture, by artist Stephen Broadbent, and depicts the encounter of the woman of Samaria with Jesus, as described in John 4:5–15. It is sculpted in bronze and is located in the cloister gardens at Chester Cathedral.

The image, I suggest, is rich in allusions to aspects of Receptive Ecumenism, with the potential to draw the viewer in to what may be needed, and elicited, in regard to disposition, relationships and behaviour when choosing that way of Receptive Ecumenism.

Especially, it hints at the fruitfulness for faith and life that may flow from engaging with Receptive Ecumenism processes within any setting of Church.

The following meditation is offered as a tool for reading before and after each paper in this publication, as a way of imaginatively letting words and concepts be imbued in the heart, mind and actions of the reader.

*   *   *

The woman and Christ, while quite distinct, are joined together as a continuous piece, and the two figures face one another. Together they hold a bowl of water, and they arise, seemingly, from a basin of water, around which are the words: 'Jesus said "the water that I shall give will be an inner spring always welling up for eternal life"' (Jn 4:14).

The sculpture is outdoors, in the midst of nature, and located on land that would generally be described as holy ground: the grounds of a cathedral, where people have gathered for worship and for life for over 1,000 years. Yet, it is also an open space into which anyone may enter.

I invite you to imagine that you are in those grounds, approaching the sculpture.

What is it that you feel? What do you notice?

The sculpture is vulnerable to the elements, and to the eyes of all who pass, or linger. For some there may be surprise at the depiction of such intimacy between a man and a woman, between Christ and a woman, in such a place. It might be disquieting, as though intruding on something that is private or out of place.

You can walk around the image and view it from various angles, and in the changing light of day and night some aspects will appear to be obscured, and others will become more fully illuminated.

While the gardens will change with the seasons, and people will come and go throughout the year, the two figures will remain constant, faithful to one another.

There is a safety railing around the water from which the two figures seem to arise. There is a gate, however, that would enable one to enter—and to leave. What would it take for you to open the gate, step through and into the surrounding water—courage, or curiosity, or yearning to be closer to the image and the story?

Walking around the figures, you can draw close to them and can touch them.

The outside edge of the water basin in which the figures 'stand' has the following words inscribed, 'Jesus said "the water that I shall give will be an inner spring always welling up for eternal life"' (Jn 4:14).

There is a sense of the two figures emerging and rising from the water, from the same source—the water of life, the waters of baptism.

The woman appears to rise from and with Christ, and Christ forms a firm base for the woman to soar above. All the while, they are fully connected to one another, and to the water.

Neither the woman nor Christ dominates—rather, both appear to be holding the other, and to being held by the other at the same time.

The image is both solid and open: there is space between the figures and space around the figures. The large middle space between the bodies is what could be described as heart-shaped, and the space between the upper body and the two heads forms a smaller heart-shape in reverse. These reveal a relationship that embraces openness and a listening with the heart.

Both figures are cast from the one material, unified yet unique.

They are joined to one another, facing one another, close to each other—yet with space between and for one another, making space for the other, and space for more, and more.

The eyes are fixed firmly on one another, trusting and loving one another, respectful and attentive.

Intense, yet tender.

The two figures seem totally absorbed by one another. Intimate, even. Eyes gaze on one another, not distracted by the world, yet fully in the world.

It is circular without sharp edges, and conveys gentleness, strength and love.

It is both static, yet dynamic.

Both figures hold the bowl . . . not separately but hands around the hands of the other, being held by the other, gently yet firmly, safely . . . who is giving, and who is receiving?

The bowl runs over with water, with life, returning to the source, and being gathered up again.

The bowl is overflowing, and the garments appear like a chrysalis, promising that abundance and beauty are about to emerge.

It is time to return to the world. In walking again through the water and heading towards the gate, you turn around briefly to look back at the image. And the realization dawns that the whole sculpture looks like it could tip over at any time, and roll through—or over—the gate, to who knows where, with who knows what possibilities.

There is little doubt that the woman will never again go anywhere without Christ—and Christ will be going nowhere without her. Each is vulnerable, yet each is totally trusting of the other, going where they will, gaining in abundance, flourishing in life and becoming more today than they were yesterday.

* * *

As you read the papers in this publication, whenever you explore the way of Receptive Ecumenism, and talk about it with others, may the remembrance of this image evoke easily some of the characteristics that Receptive Ecumenism needs and elicits—courage, vulnerability, humility, openness, trust, gentleness, abundance, love and communion—with Christ and with one another.

A Forum for Theology in the World Vol 5 No 2/2018

'Neither Greek nor Jew . . . for Christ is all and in all' (Col 3:11–17) A Bible Study

Vicky Balabanski

---

[11] Here there is neither Greek nor Jew, circumcised or uncircumcised, barbarian, Scythian, slave[8] or free, but Christ is all and in all.
[12] Therefore, as the elect of God, holy and dearly loved, clothe yourselves with a heart of mercy, kindness, humility, gentleness, and patience, [13] bearing with one another and forgiving one another, if someone happens to have a complaint against anyone else. Just as the Lord has forgiven you, so you also forgive others.
[14] And to all these virtues add love, which is the perfect bond. [15] Let the peace of Christ be in control in your heart (for you were in fact called as one body[17] to this peace), and be thankful. [16] Let the word of Christ[18] dwell in you richly, teaching and exhorting one another with all wisdom, singing psalms, hymns, and spiritual songs, all with grace[19] in your hearts to God. [17] And whatever you do in word or deed, do it all in the name of the Lord Jesus, giving thanks to God the Father through him (Col 3:11–17 NET).

I wonder whether you have ever been to a place where people's clothes tell a detailed story about their identity?

The clothes we put on this morning do say something about each of us—whether we like to be formal or more casual, whether we like to be comfortable or warm or smart or sophisticated, or whether we don't give it a second thought. Something about our personality is perhaps apparent in those choices.

But there are places in the world where one's clothing not only hints at one's identity, but proclaims it; be it a religious, political, cultural or kinship identity.

I visited Varanasi in India a few years ago. It is a very ancient city, one of the oldest in the world, a spiritual capital in India; the place where Buddhism was founded. Walking through the old city I found myself wondering about all the different people and their distinctive clothes. There were Hindus, Buddhists, Jains, Muslims and Christians, there were castes and classes and categories on display. There was a highly nuanced social script being played out visually, a script I could not read or interpret. Coming from a culture that is rather wary of social distinction based on clothes, this was a fascinating glimpse into a culture that lives and breathes the visual display of difference.

I suspect that first century Asia Minor and the thriving Lycus Valley cities like Colossae, with their prosperous trade routes, were much more like Varanasi than a contemporary Western city. There would have been Greeks wearing the linen *chiton* and the heavier *himation* as a cloak; Roman men with their toga communicating their power and prestige; Roman women draped with a *stola* as a sign of respectability and tradition.[1] There were barbarians with their pointed beards and trousers,[2] there were fierce Scythian horsemen and women in their padded leggings, indigenous Phrygians with their pointed caps, there were Jews with their fringed garments, and of course slaves with their short garments and exposed legs. One's clothing and style could also say something about belonging to a philosophical school.

This part of the world was famous for its soft black wool. It also knew the value of distinctive colours and dyes, from the Tyrian purple of the murex shell to the distinctive stripes on Roman tunics denoting senatorial rank.[3] So much of one's identity was displayed visually: ethnic origin, gender, political status, rank and office, and philosophical affiliation were proclaimed visually. Your clothes proclaimed your identity.

The passage from Colossians 3 quoted above invokes this link between the way you dress and your true identity: '. . . clothe yourselves with a heart of mercy, kindness, humility, gentleness, and patience' (3:12).

Paul and Timothy are named as co-authors of Colossians. With the help of Epaphras, whom they called their 'beloved fellow-slave'

---

1. Rosemary Canavan, *Clothing the Body of Christ at Colossae: A Visual Construction of Identity*, WUNT, 2, 334, (Tübingen: Mohr Siebeck, 2012), 130.
2. Canavan, *Clothing the Body of Christ*, 123.
3. Canavan, *Clothing the Body of Christ*, 3.

(Col 1:7), they were writing to a fledgling Christian community they had not met in person (Col 2:1). I am going to refer to Timothy as the primary author of our passage. I have argued elsewhere that there is a strong case that Paul was alive and co-authored this letter, particularly in the opening and closing sections.[4] Subtle developments in the language and ideas of the rest of the letter also suggest that we should take seriously the co-authorship that the opening of Colossians names (Col 1:1).

Colossians 3 uses the image of clothing to speak about the Colossian believers' new identity in Christ. Clothing is a wonderful metaphor to convey the change of allegiance and identity that these believers chose as they embraced the Gospel. There were things to lay aside—behaviours and ways of thinking and speaking that marked their old identity—and things to consciously take on—compassion, kindness, humility, meekness and patience. For the believers in Colossae, schooled as they were in the subtleties of visual identity markers, the idea of displaying their new identity, not by clothes but by their behaviour and speech, would have both resonated with them and challenged them.

'Clothing yourself with Christ' was a metaphor that Paul had used in one of his earliest letters, the letter to the Galatians (Gal 3:27). There, it was explicitly linked with baptism, where you lay aside your old self and clothe yourself with the new, like putting on a baptismal garment. Here in Colossians 3 we meet the metaphor again, extended and shaped to make the ethical qualities of the new life more apparent. The baptismal link with clothing is not explicit in Colossians, though it hovers there for anyone who knows the Letter to the Galatians. And baptism has already been invoked in Colossians; the metaphor that Timothy used in chapter 2 is of baptism as a 'spiritual circumcision' (Col 2:11–12), in response to the Colossians, who like the Galatians a decade or so earlier, were keen on the idea of physical circumcision, in addition to their baptism, and keen on becoming full Jewish proselytes.

The Colossian believers appear to have been very attracted to establishing their identity alongside other social groups; to aligning

---

4. Vicky Balabanski, 'Where is Philemon? The Case for a Logical Fallacy in the Correlation of the Data in Philemon and Colossians 1.1–2; 4.7–18', in *Journal for the Study of the New Testament,* 38/2 (2015): 131–50.

themselves closely with their Jewish neighbours in relation to food and drink, festivals, new moons and Sabbaths (Col 2:16), circumcision (Col 2:11–13) and purity practices (Col 2:21). It seems that they wanted to establish their identity as Christ-believers as though they were simply a subset of Judaism, alongside all the other social sets and subsets.

The metaphor of clothing confronts the Colossians believers with a radical, and maybe shocking idea about their identity in Christ. They could dress like anyone they met in the streets, and still be true to Christ! They could dress like Greeks or Jews, like proselytes or pagans, like Barbarians or even like Scythians (the fiercest and most barbaric of all the peoples!)—they could all be true Christ followers as long as their *inner clothing* were compassion, kindness, humility, meekness and patience.

The clothing metaphor is a really challenging one. It confronts perceptions of insiders and outsiders. This metaphor says that Christ, the very image of the unseen God and the One through whom all things are created and sustained—Christ can be the Lord of Greeks as well as Jews, the uncircumcised as well as the circumcised, slave as well as free, Lord not only of the Barbarians but even of the Scythians! Christ is truly the Lord of the cosmos who lays claim to all peoples, whatever their culture, their status or rank. So it pushes us to see that there are no limits to those whom the God of the universe, visible in Christ, can call and equip. Never assume that the pagans—whether they be Greeks, the uncircumcised, Barbarians or Scythians—are outside the scope of the universal love of Christ! One can even say about outsiders: Christ is all and in all!

Christ is all and in all. The ability to see Christ in all and indeed Christ *as* all must be part of the new life, the new perception with which we clothe ourselves. This is not possible, humanly speaking, unless we lean into the Spirit of God and allow that unifying, clarifying, grace-filled perception to take hold of us. Christ is all and in all. This is truly a mystery.

The second aspect of this provocative metaphor of clothing is not just to do with outward perception, but how one thinks about oneself. This teaching challenges believers to reject outward identity-markers of clothing and circumcision, and instead to show the inner identity markers of behaviour and disposition. If Christ is all and in all, we don't need to differentiate ourselves with the outer markers. At the same time, if outward markers of ethnicity or other affiliation are not as central as we thought, we don't have to treat them as though they were ultimate barriers to our unity in Christ. We don't have to all be the same. Christ-believers can wear the toga, a long or a short tunic, Christ-believers can wear leggings and various caps. The outward markers are relativised when Christ is all and in all.

This seems to me to be a significant teaching as we explore the implications of receptive ecumenism. How do we think about our distinctive practices and traditions—our cultural and religious identities? In our time and place we may no longer worry so much about clothes or indeed ecclesiastical vestments or other identity markers—we may in fact celebrate ethnic differences. But when it comes to denominational affiliation, do we have the Spirit-inspired eyes to perceive Christ as all and in all?

Take a moment to picture someone from another and very different Christian tradition to your own. You might like to close your eyes as you do this exercise. Just a single person will do, or you may wish to imagine a very different Christian community at worship. Hold that image as we hear the words of Colossians 3:11 again: Christ is all and in all.

Back in 1996 my husband Peter and I were living in Jerusalem. We had the chance to celebrate Orthodox Christmas Eve at the Church of the Nativity in Bethlehem. After two hours waiting to pass through the security cordon, we finally got into the church towards midnight. We wove our way through the crowd, all made up of different congregations.

To our left were the Copts; clergy at their altar, singing lustily, the congregation crammed in around them and joining in the responses. To our right, the Syrians, gathered around another altar were doing the same thing—and singing at the tops of *their* voices. Ahead of us, other congregations were contributing their hymns to the general ambience. It was quite something!

But if all that weren't enough, the Greek congregation chose that moment to begin their three-fold procession around the entire church. Down from the main sanctuary they came, with a vanguard of burly, robed monks singing powerfully as they made a passage through the crowd and formed a cordon around the Patriarch and his entourage. And they were all singing too. The head of their very long procession was about a verse or two out of time with the rear. So from where we stood, the overall effect was extraordinary to say the least. Cacophony's the word that springs to mind.

It was just then that we happened to see Yazeed, a young Palestinian Christian friend, standing nearby. He was beaming from ear to ear. We went over to him to ask what the joke was—had a torch-bearer almost singed a bishop's beard or something? But no. There was no joke.

> 'This is wonderful!' he said.
> 'Wonderful?'
> 'Yes; this is what I always imagine heaven must be like.
> 'What?'
> 'Yes; everybody praising God in their own language, all at the same time.'
> Christ is all, and in all.

I would like to spend the next few minutes exploring some aspects of our passage in the light of this overarching insight of Christ as all and in all.

'Here there is neither Greek nor Jew, circumcised or uncircumcised, barbarian, Scythian, slave or free, but Christ is all and in all.' This is both a very familiar and strangely jarring version of this Pauline teaching. We can compare Colossians 3:11 to the similar verse in Galatians 3:28: 'There is neither Jew nor Greek, there is neither slave nor free, there is neither male nor female—for all of you are one in Christ Jesus.'

When we put these two verses alongside each other, we may find ourselves frustrated that Timothy has changed an important aspect of the Pauline saying in Galatians, namely there is no mention here of male and female. Adding to our concern about this change, the passage that immediately follows our passage in Colossians is the earliest of the household codes. These sets of rules are found in the later New Testament writings and seem to sanctify a Greco-Roman household order and urge wives to be subject to their husbands.

There may be several things going on here. There were only about ten or twelve intervening years since Paul had written that radically inclusive baptismal saying in Galatians 3:28 which in Christ flagged the irrelevance of gender divisions. But a lot had been taking place since then. Margaret McDonald points out there were strong ascetic currents taking hold in various parts of the church. In Corinth, people had started downplaying any difference between the genders, dressing androgynously and rejecting the need for marriage.[5] Paul had not anticipated the Corinthians taking his original baptismal proclamation quite so literally! When he subsequently wrote a baptismal saying to the Corinthians, he left out the male and female categories: 'For in the one Spirit we were all baptised into one body—Jews or Greeks, slaves or free—and were all made to drink of one Spirit' (1 Cor 12:13 NRSV). The Corinthian experiences had made Paul and Timothy more cautious about how to express the boundary-breaking reality of Christ.

In Colossians 3, everyone is urged to clothe themselves the same way—in compassion, kindness, humility, meekness and patience. The 'coat' above all these things must be love. This metaphor may be about 'inner clothing', but it should have an outward impact. This sort of clothing could look and perhaps *should* look androgynous, with both men and women putting on the same qualities. It's only after setting up what should be the disposition of all believers that Timothy draws particular attention to certain aspects of the exhortation for particular groups: wives, remember your humility and patience; husbands, remember your love and your gentleness; children and slaves, don't forget your obedience; Masters, don't neglect the justice and fairness.

We might wonder whether these exhortations re-establish the very divisions that the grand vision of Christ has broken down. The reception history of the household codes would suggest that they often have done just that. I suspect that in the wake of their Corinthian experience, Timothy and Paul felt it necessary to specify that they were not pronouncing the abolition of the traditional family. Instead, in using a household code they are picking up a traditional Greek way of saying that clothing oneself in Christ might look different for diverse members of the Christian household.

Differences between believers in terms of gender, age and status may well have different challenges for putting on this Christ-like clothing. That might well be true, particularly in a hierarchical society such as Paul and Timothy lived in. What a shame that the household code which followed our passage has overshadowed the unisex clothing metaphor and has been used to sacralise and perpetuate

---

5. Margaret Y McDonald, *Colossians and Ephesians*, Sacra Pagina 17 (Collegeville, MI: Michael Glazier/Liturgical Press, 2000), 145–8.

a hierarchical society! All the more reason for us to insist that the household codes have a literary and a cultural context. The literary context of Colossians 3 shows us that the overarching teaching for all Christians is to clothe ourselves in compassion, kindness, humility, meekness and patience, and above all, with love.

It occurs to me that by calling those teachings 'household codes', or *Haustafeln,* or household rules, we seem to be fixing them as immutable codes. What if they went by a different heading in our Bibles that indicates their connection with the Christ-like clothing which exhorts every believer equally? What about a heading like 'Customizing the garment for service'? Just a thought!

I have spent some time on this aspect of our passage, because each of our church traditions mirrors formative historical contexts for understanding the role of women, of children, and of men, as well as of slaves and their owners. I hope that in the context of receptive ecumenism, we can revisit the radical baptismal formulas of the Pauline tradition and hear again that Christ is all and in all.

Our passage gives a primary role to forgiveness: we are to bear with one another and forgive one another, just as the Lord has forgiven us. I hear a strong echo of the Lord's Prayer here. Forgiveness is one of the most counter-cultural things we can do—and one of the most Christ-like. It stands out in our cultural landscape as an identity marker that can baffle and intrigue the secular world. If we are connected with one another as people who have been forgiven, then we can be connected as people who also forgive.

The passage calls on believers to 'let the peace of Christ rule in our hearts'. We live at a time when anxiety is one of the most prevalent and disabling realities that people face—political, economic, relational, and personal—anxiety is everywhere. What might it look like to allow the peace of Christ to rule in our hearts, and not just in our hearts, but in our corporate structures as well?

One of the answers that our passage gives is that a close accompaniment to experiencing the peace of Christ is the disposition of thankfulness. Gratitude. If we cultivate a disposition of thankfulness, we remember that everything is not up to us. Every good thing is ultimately God's, and every difficult thing is ultimately in God's hands. In that knowledge and in that wisdom we can be thankful.

As our passages moves towards its conclusion, it calls on believers to 'let the word of Christ dwell in you richly, teaching and exhorting one another with all wisdom, singing psalms, hymns, and spiritual songs'. The word of Christ is something that can dwell inside us richly, like a delicious and sustaining meal. One way of allowing that to happen is as we worship together. Timothy already knew, as we know today, that the songs we sing together shape us long after the worshipping community has dispersed. I am intrigued by the three categories of song that are named here: psalms and hymns and spiritual songs. It's almost as though our different styles of worship are anticipated and affirmed here: the biblical psalms, the composed hymns and the contemporary, more charismatic songs. All of them can be ways of shaping ourselves into communities where the word of Christ dwells richly, and where we teach and get alongside each other as we attend to learning more of the wisdom of God.

The final seal on all of this is the call to do all these things in the name of the Lord Jesus, giving thanks to God through him. Our church traditions have developed ways of doing this as a seal to every prayer—in Jesus' name, for Jesus' sake, through Jesus Christ our Lord. It is good to remember that our liturgical traditions have been shaped by those who let the word of Christ dwell in them richly.

We have been reflecting together on this ancient scriptural passage as people from many contexts and traditions. What binds us together is our common allegiance to the Lord Jesus Christ. Our denominational identity markers are important, but they are not the most significant thing about us. We are followers of Christ, who is all and in all. Knowing that, we can delight in the diversity of the people around us, connecting with one another as people who have already been forgiven and who give glory to God according to our own distinctive ways of worship and theology. Let us grow as people who are open to learning more from one another about the key inner identity markers—compassion, kindness, humility, meekness and patience—so that together we may flourish more fully in Christ as a sign of God's love for our world.

Bibliography

Balabanski, Vicky, 'Where is Philemon? The Case for a Logical Fallacy in the Correlation of the Data in Philemon and Colossians 1.1–2; 4.7–18', in *Journal for the Study of the New Testament*, 38/2 (2015): 131–50.

Canavan, Rosemary, *Clothing the Body of Christ at Colossae: A Visual Construction of Identity*, Wissenschaftliche Untersuchungen zum Neuen Testament, II, 334, (Tübingen: Mohr Siebeck, 2012).

McDonald, Margaret Y, *Colossians and Ephesians*, Sacra Pagina 17 (Collegeville, MI: Michael Glazier/Liturgical Press, 2000).

Creation Eagerly Waits for the Children of God to be Revealed (Rom 8:18–30) A Bible Study

Vicky Balabanski

[18] I consider that the sufferings of this present time are not worth comparing with the glory about to be revealed to us. [19] For the creation waits with eager longing for the revealing of the children of God; [20] for the creation was subjected to futility, not of its own will but by the will of the one who subjected it, in hope [21] that the creation itself will be set free from its bondage to decay and will obtain the freedom of the glory of the children of God.

[22] We know that the whole creation has been groaning in labour pains until now; [23] and not only the creation, but we ourselves, who have the first fruits of the Spirit, groan inwardly while we wait for adoption, the redemption of our body.

[24] For in hope we were saved. Now hope that is seen is not hope. For who hopes for what is seen? [25] But if we hope for what we do not see, we wait for it with patience.

[26] Likewise the Spirit helps us in our weakness; for we do not know how to pray as we ought, but that very Spirit intercedes with sighs too deep for words.

[27] And God, who searches the heart, knows what is the mind of the Spirit, because the Spirit intercedes for the saints according to the will of God.

[28] We know that all things work together for good for those who love God, who are called according to his purpose. [29] For those whom he foreknew he also predestined to be conformed to the image of his Son, in order that he might be the firstborn within a large family. [30] And those whom he predestined he also called; and those whom he called he also justified; and those whom he justified he also glorified (Rom 8:18–30 NRSV).

In this passage, Paul articulates a deep longing—longing for the world to be as it should be, longing for the children of God to live up to their vocation, longing for every person, indeed every creature, to experience fullness of life and communion in God's good creation. He frames this longing in the language both of conviction and hope—not only that God shares our longing, but the Spirit is actively prompting and propelling us towards this hope. Our role is not to generate the hope, but to lean into the Spirit and find ourselves propelled towards that horizon.

Leaning into the Spirit is an evocative image; like a sailing boat where the crew put on harnesses and lean back into the wind so that they can counterbalance the forces on the vessel and speed over the waves. Leaning into the Spirit. To me it says something about trust, about deciding to relax into a moving flow of wind that could overwhelm us if we were rigid, but as we lean, we experience the exhilaration of being caught up in something much greater than ourselves. It also says something about confidence as well—confidence that we are part of a bigger picture. And it's a relational image too—you lean into someone when you know that they won't let you fall.

I want to explore this passage as it shapes our vision of receptive ecumenism under three headings: Creation, the Spirit and the Children of God.

I want to begin, though, by recognising that this is a difficult passage. We know in general terms that this is a vision of eschatological liberation and renewal. But it is a passage with many implicit links that Paul confidently expected his recipients to grasp.

Paul writes 'we know' twice within these few verses, as though he expected the Roman believers to know the details of the backstory. We do not necessarily know what those first Roman churches knew, and so as we listen carefully to this vision of restoration and renewal, we need to fill in some of the connecting lines. So that is the first reason why this is a challenging passage.

The second reason that it is challenging is that alongside humanity and the Spirit of God, we also find another active player or protagonist, namely creation. In these verses we find creation waiting with eager longing and groaning in labour pains—as much a living *subject* as any human being, and one whose eschatological future is inextricably bound together with that of the children of God. It seems that the story of redemption is greater than a story of God and humanity—it has a cosmic scope, with God creating and reconciling all things. Creation's role in the big-picture story of God's salvation is intriguing.

A third challenging aspect of this passage is that it refers to God's people in a variety of ways: the 'children of God' who need to be revealed, those who 'love God', those who are 'predestined', called, justified and ultimately to be glorified. All of these ways of describing God's people are not neatly defined or categorised—we cannot easily say, ah yes, we know who those people are. There is a breadth and a mystery to who the children of God are who will be revealed, and for whom the creation waits with eager longing.

A fourth challenge is in verse 28: 'We know that all things work together for good for those who love God, who are called according to his purpose.' This is a difficult verse. Even with the most fervent belief in God's sovereignty, how could natural disasters, the abuse of children or the destruction of the environment be 'for good'? I want to give some attention to this verse as well.

There is a story being articulated in these verses, even if it's not one that we can easily grasp. David Horrell, Professor of New Testament in Exeter, puts it this way:

> Pauline thought cannot be conveyed as a series of propositions to be 'believed', but only as a story which is 'lived, retold and embodied in the practices of the community which celebrates that story.'[1]

This story is the story of the *missio Dei*—the story of the gracious, salvific movement of God reconciling the world to Godself. The importance of living, telling and embodying the story is that it's the big picture that we all share. This is not a denominational tale, but the mission of God writ large that embraces all of us. I want to explore this big picture, this metanarrative, under three headings: creation, the Spirit and the children of God.

---

1. David Horrell, Cherryl Hunt and Christopher Southgate, *Greening Paul: Rereading the Apostle in a Time of Ecological Crisis* (Waco, TX: Baylor University Press. 2010), 58.

Creation

We have heard that Pauline thought is like a story—always implicit in Paul's letters, but never articulated in full. We might think that the role of creation in this passage is an isolated phenomenon, like an island in a vast ocean. But actually such an island indicates something deeper about the ocean bed. More recently Pauline scholars are coming to recognise that creation is not tangential to the central narrative of salvation, but that this 'island' is connected with the deeper structures of Paul's thought.[2]

Cosmic liberation and renewal is something that concerns not only God and humanity, but *all things*, all creation. We know from the account of creation in Genesis 3 that the fate and future of non-human creation are inextricably bound up with the fate and future of humanity. The hubris and deception that led to the alienation between humans and God also led to the alienation between humans and creation. This brings to mind the words in Genesis 3:17–19: 'Cursed is the ground because of you; in toil you shall eat of it . . . thorns and thistles it shall bring forth for you . . . by the sweat of your face you shall eat bread until you return to the ground, for out of it you were taken. You are dust and to dust you shall return.' That part of the story was well known to Paul's recipients, and is reflected when he writes about creation being 'subjected to futility, not of its own will but by the will of the one who subjected it.' Creation was caught up in the human mess, not by its own choice or culpability, and the result was 'futility': toil, thorns and thistles, sweat and death.

What Paul's audience in Rome may not have known is that in thinking about this back story, Paul is not thinking about creation as a passive recipient. Here in Romans 8, creation is not simply a grudging and punishing producer of thorns and thistles. Instead, creation is an active and generous subject leaning together with humans towards a shared future of freedom and glory: '. . . creation waits with eager

---

2. Richard Hays, *The Faith of Jesus Christ: The Narrative Substructure of Galatians 3:1–4:11*, second edition (Grand Rapids, MI: Eerdmans, 2002), 33–117; Edward Adams, 'Paul's Story of God and Creation: The Story of How God Fulfils His Purposes in Creation', in *Narrative Dynamics in Paul: A Critical Assessment,* edited by Bruce W Longenecker (Louisville, KY: Westminster/John Knox Press, 2002), 19–43; Sigve Tonstad, 'Creation Groaning in Labor Pains' in *Exploring Ecological Hermeneutics* edited by Norman C Habel and Peter Trudinger (Atlanta: Society of Biblical Literature. 2008), 141–9.

longing for the revealing of the children of God . . .' and 'the creation itself will be set free from its bondage to decay and will obtain the freedom of the glory of the children of God.' Creation is depicted not as our enemy, but as our active partner and supporter. Cosmic liberation and renewal concerns not only God and humanity, but all things, all creation.

Thinking about creation as an active and generous subject is not the easiest thing to do. After all, we are schooled into thinking of nature as being all about competition and the survival of the fittest. But science is beginning to show us a different picture. I have been enjoying reading a book by Peter Wohlleben called *The Hidden Life of Trees: What they feel, How they communicate.*[3] It turns out that trees are social beings, creating social networks, supporting their own species and even other species, communicating danger, and equalizing nutrients in a kind of social security system. Wohlleben describes how as a young forester he was expected to girdle or ring bark forest beeches, removing a three-foot wide strip of bark all around the trunk to make room for others to grow.[4] What he came to discover was that the healthy trees fought hard to help the damaged ones survive. Through the network of roots and fungi that the forest shares, quite a few of the trees that had that three-foot wide strip of bark removed all around the trunk survive to this day. Wohlleben marvels at what the community of trees can do. For me this is an example of the mysterious and wonderful interconnectedness of creation. We think that it's all about competition, but in fact, in God's Wisdom, there is a parallel and perhaps more fundamental story at work of co-operation and care at work even now. The longed-for liberation and renewal of the cosmos is a renewal and triumph of that story, and concerns not only God and humanity, but all things, all creation.

I want to say a few words at this point about that difficult verse 28, which speaks about all things working for good for those who love God. Paul has been writing in this passage about the positive connection between humanity and 'all things'; creation longs for the revealing of God's children, and it groans together with us in labour pains as it waits to share our freedom. Here in verse 28, Paul elaborates

---

3. Peter Wohlleben, *The Hidden Life of Trees: What they Feel, How they Communicate,* translated by Jane Billinghurst (Carlton, VIC: Black Inc, 2016).
4. Wohlleben, *The Hidden Life of Trees,* 17–18.

further. He says: 'We know that—for those who love God—all things (*panta*) work together for good.' Often we take this to mean that every *event* is for good. But I don't think that's what Paul means here. 'All things' does not mean all events, but 'all creation', which groans and labours with us for good towards a shared future. This picks up a theme in the Wisdom tradition that creation mysteriously works for the good of God's people:

> Wisdom 16:24 For creation, serving you who made it, exerts itself to punish the unrighteous, and in kindness relaxes on behalf of those who trust in you.

> Wisdom 19:6 For the whole creation in its nature was fashioned anew, complying with your commands, so that your children might be kept unharmed.

So we have an active partner leaning with us towards God's future, namely creation. In the context of receptive ecumenism, it seems to me that the recent encyclical of Pope Francis called *Laudato si'* is a profoundly ecumenical vision of reconciliation and renewal of all things.[5] As we, the people of God, look beyond our own boundaries and glimpse the big picture of the *missio Dei*, we find a much clearer vision of what really matters to God. Creation, alongside the poor and oppressed, really matters to God. The glorious freedom of the children of God for which creation longs involves liberation from injustice and transformative participation in the life of God.[6] This embraces not only the human condition, but the liberation and renewal of all things.

Spirit

Let's turn now to what this passage has to say about the Spirit. The Spirit is very prominent in this passage, particular in verses 23, 26 and 27. Paul writes that just as creation is groaning in labour pains, and

---

5. *Laudato si'*: On Care for Our Common Home, <http://w2.vatican.va/content/dam/francesco/pdf/encyclicals/documents/papa-francesco_20150524_enciclica-laudato-si_en.pdf>. Accessed 17/04/2018.
6. Michael Gorman, *Becoming the Gospel: Paul, Participation, and Mission* (Grand Rapids, MI: Eerdmans, 2015), 225.

humanity is groaning in anticipation of liberation, so too, the Spirit of God is groaning with us (v 26). The translation 'sighs too deep for words' obscures the fact that the Spirit is also groaning. So this passage describes a three-fold groaning—creation groans in verse 22, we who have the first fruits of the Spirit groan (v 23), and the Spirit groans with us in verse 26. The groans can be both groans of lament for the suffering of the world, and also groans of anticipation. Labour pains are like that—both pain and anticipation of release. There is something profoundly Spirit-inspired in groaning for a better world. We share this longing with all those who grieve for the suffering of the world and who work to alleviate that suffering. The Spirit is alongside us in this process of bringing God's future to birth. The Spirit awakens and sustains that hope for the future, giving us courage to face the present.

There is a very practical aspect to the work of the Spirit which we meet in this passage. It says: 'Likewise the Spirit helps us in our weakness; for we do not know how to pray as we ought, but that very Spirit intercedes with sighs too deep for words' (v 26). Likewise the Spirit helps us in our weakness; for we do not know how to pray as we ought, but that very Spirit intercedes with sighs too deep for words.

It is as though the Spirit is awakening and sustaining that longing for a restored future that we hardly know how to articulate or even hope for. The Spirit is accompanying us in this time of waiting and hoping, reminding us that God's horizon is bigger than ours. The Spirit is enabling us to pray.

As we seek to lean into the Spirit over these days, we are reminded to trust that God is calling us to long for the reconciliation and renewal of all things. We are borne forward with God's own momentum. Our hope is generated and sustained by the divine Life of God, and communicated to us through the Holy Spirit.

We hear of that Divine Life explicitly in verse 27: And God, who searches the heart, knows what is the mind of the Spirit, because the Spirit intercedes for the saints according to the will of God.

There is a reciprocal, centripetal and perichoretic movement described here that draws us into the purposes of God.

As I think about the movement of the Spirit, I am reminded that God implanted the seed of the Gospel before missionary work took place. This is something that the Uniting Church in Australia has come to recognise in relation to the UAICC, the Uniting Aboriginal and Islander Christian Congress. Some years ago the UAICC and the Uniting Church went through a process of drafting a Preamble to the Church's constitution, which acknowledges that the Holy Spirit was at work prior to European settlement. Paragraph 3 of that Preamble reads:

> The First Peoples had already encountered the Creator God before the arrival of the colonisers; the Spirit was already in the land revealing God to the people through law, custom and ceremony. The same love and grace that was finally and fully revealed in Jesus Christ sustained the First Peoples and gave them particular insights into God's ways.

Notice what is said here, and what is not said. This affirms that the Holy Spirit was already at work in Australia over the millennia prior to white settlement, and that the Spirit's work left its imprint in the law, custom and ceremony of the Aboriginal people. It does not say that every aspect of these laws was fully correlated with God's purposes—the full and final revelation of God's love and grace was revealed in Jesus Christ. Nevertheless, the Holy Spirit was already shaping the people of this land.

I saw that first-hand recently when I attended a funeral in a remote Aboriginal community. We have an Aboriginal daughter, and her father passed away this year. Attending the funeral of Kumantjai was a remarkable experience. I had never been to a funeral where the whole community sat attentive for hours, not moving away to eat or have a cup of tea, but grieving the loss, sometimes out loud with tears and wailing, but for long stretches with a stillness that seemed to me to be Spirit-inspired. This was a Christian service, but shaped by law, custom and ceremony. It was a privilege to be there. The Holy Spirit draws us into the life of God, and enables us to grieve, to pray and to be shaped as channels of God's momentum towards a better world.

The Children of God

So we have thought about creation, we have thought about the Spirit, and now I want to think a little more about the nature of the people of God as described in this passage. I said earlier that this passage refers to God's people in a variety of ways: the 'children of God', who need to be revealed, those who 'love God', those who are predestined, called, justified and ultimately to be glorified. All these ways of describing

God's people are not neatly defined or categorised. There is a breadth and a mystery to who these children of God are who will be revealed. I like that. Just as God is greater and more mysterious than we can imagine, so too, the children of God are more diverse and more mysterious than we might think.

Part of what it means to be the children of God has something to do with glory. Remember that the passage opens with these words about glory. 'I consider that the sufferings of this present time are not worth comparing with the *glory* about to be revealed to us' (v 18).

Or 'into us' (εἰς ἡμᾶς)! This is not simply a cognitive thing, but participation in the glory of God. Humanity's sin means that we have forfeited the glory of God, as Paul made clear earlier in this letter: 'all have sinned and fall short of the glory of God' (Rom 3:23); we have 'exchanged the glory of the immortal God for images resembling a mortal human being or birds or four-footed animals or reptiles' (Rom 1:23). We have refused to give God the glory, and so have forfeited our own.

According to Paul, creation's and humanity's plight is like a loop or spiral. Humanity's refusal to give God the glory is *the* root of our enslavement to sin.[7] It also distorts our perception of things, too, so that we end up worshipping the creature rather than the Creator (Rom 1:19–28). Our distorted perception of creation is also a *self-limitation*, in the sense of that it obscures the glory of God *in us*. Of ourselves we are unable to exit this spiral. Only God can bring about the liberation and renewal of the cosmos, restoring the glory to its rightful place—not to the creature but to God, and restoring the image of that glory in us. It is for that reason that the creation waits with eager longing for the children of God to be revealed—a revealing of the glory of humanity means a revealing of a restored relationship between God, creation and humanity.

So the children of God have a central part to play in the big picture of God, according to Paul. As he has stated earlier in the letter:

> Therefore, since we are justified by faith, we have peace with God through our Lord Jesus Christ, [2] through whom we have obtained access to this grace in which we stand; and we boast in our hope of sharing the glory of God (Rom 5:1–2).

---

7. Beverly Roberts Gaventa, 'Neither Height nor Depth: Discerning the Cosmology of Romans', in *Scottish Journal of Theology*, 64/3 (2011): 268.

Through Jesus we are set right with God, given access to the wonderful grace of God, and can hope to share in God's glory. We will finally be restored to full participation in the life of God, conformed to the image of God's Son, part of a large family. These are some of the words that our passage uses to describe this future glory. No one set of words can fully convey this vision.

One way of describing this participation in the life of God is the concept of *theosis*. This concept of ever-increasing participation in the Divine Life is something that goes back to the Cappadocian fathers and mothers, and is being increasingly recovered and explored in circles not limited just to the Orthodox tradition.[8] From very different contexts and traditions, the concept of *theosis*—of being drawn into the Divine Life—is being recognised as key to sharing God's glory. This has great potential for receptive ecumenical discussion.

One final observation: Paul says we are waiting for adoption, the redemption of our body (v 23). Cosmic liberation is not redemption *from* the body, but the redemption *of* the body. Notice that this says the redemption of our body, not bodies. The singular suggests that this is not just about individual resurrection bodies, but about the corporate body—the body of Christ, finally revealed as the source not just of believers but of all things (1 Cor 8:6). In the end, Christ is all and in all, as we saw in the Colossians study above.

It may perhaps seem strange to focus on the big picture of our eschatological hope in the context of reflecting on receptive ecumenism. I trust that my reason for doing so has become clear, namely to situate ourselves against the big picture of God's salvation, and see ourselves in all our diversity as part of the longed-for children of God. In this big picture, the Church is not an end in itself or a holy remnant. It is part of the wider movement of God that embraces all things. In the light of the *missio Dei*, the things that divide the children of God should not co-opt all our attention, as though we could of our own volition restore the glory of God in ourselves. It is God who is restoring that glory in us, and God the Holy Spirit who helps us in our weakness and enables us to get on board with God's plans. May we allow ourselves to be shaped by the big picture of God's purposes, who is restoring all things to full participation in the life of God.

---

8. See Michael J Gorman *Inhabiting the Cruciform God: Kenosis, Justification and Theosis in Paul's Narrative Soteriology* (Grand Rapids, MI: Eerdmans, 2009), 1–8, where he lists various scholars from protestant traditions who are exploring the significance of *theosis*.

Bibliography

Adams, Edward, 'Paul's Story of God and Creation: The Story of How God Fulfils His Purposes in Creation', in *Narrative Dynamics in Paul: A Critical Assessment,* edited by Bruce W Longenecker (Louisville, KY: Westminster/John Knox Press, 2002), 19–43.

Gaventa, Beverly Roberts, 'Neither Height nor Depth: Discerning the Cosmology of Romans', in *Scottish Journal of Theology,* 64/3 (2011): 265–278.

Gorman, Michael J, *Becoming the Gospel: Paul, Participation, and Mission* (Grand Rapids, MI: Eerdmans, 2015).

Gorman, Michael J, *Inhabiting the Cruciform God: Kenosis, Justification and Theosis in Paul's Narrative Soteriology* (Grand Rapids, MI: Eerdmans, 2009).

Hays, Richard, *The Faith of Jesus Christ: The Narrative Substructure of Galatians 3:1–4:11*, second edition (Grand Rapids, MI: Eerdmans, 2002).

Horrell, David, Cherryl Hunt, Christopher Southgate, *Greening Paul: Rereading the Apostle in a Time of Ecological Crisis* (Waco, TX: Baylor University Press, 2010).

Pope Francis, *Laudato si': On Care for Our Common Home*, <http://w2.vatican.va/content/dam/francesco/pdf/encyclicals/documents/papa-francesco_20150524_enciclica-laudato-si_en.pdf>. Accessed 17/04/2018.

Tonstad, Sigve, 'Creation Groaning in Labor Pains', in *Exploring Ecological Hermeneutics*, edited by Norman C Habel and Peter Trudinger (Atlanta: Society of Biblical Literature. 2008), 141–9.

Wohlleben, Peter, *The Hidden Life of Trees: What they Feel, How they Communicate,* translated by Jane Billinghurst (Carlton, VIC: Black Inc, 2016).

A Forum for Theology in the World Vol 5 No 2/2018

Ecclesial Decision-Making: Exploring an Insight from Karl Rahner

Denis Edwards

One of the important questions in the theory and practice of receptive ecumenism concerns criteria. What is the basis on which a church might decide that something offered by another church is to be received as a gift of the Spirit? This question has already been discussed by various theologians, including Ladislas Orsy[1] and William Rusch,[2] and I have earlier suggested six criteria that might provide guidance in such ecclesial reception. The first is that what is offered can be recognised by the receiving church as an authentic expression of biblical and apostolic faith, and the closely-related second is that what is offered can be seen as leading to Christ, to faith in him and to the practice of authentic discipleship.

The third criterion is that what is offered is not opposed to the deepest self-understanding of the receiving church, while the fourth is that the proposed gift can be seen as an organic development of the life of faith of that church. The fifth criterion is that what is offered brings to the receiving church a renewed energy and life. The final criterion is that the gift is accompanied by the fruits of the Spirit—'love, joy, peace, patience, kindness, generosity, faithfulness, gentleness and self-control' (Gal 5:22).[3]

---

1. Ladislas Orsy, 'Authentic Learning and Receiving—A Search for Criteria', in *Receptive Ecumenism and the Call to Catholic Learning,* edited by Paul D Murray (Oxford: Oxford University Press, 2008), 39–51.
2. William G Rusch, *Ecumenical Reception: Its Challenge and Opportunity* (Grand Rapids, MI: Eerdmans, 2006), 54–88.
3. Denis Edwards, 'Receptive Ecumenism and the Charism of a Partner Church: The Example of Justification', in *The Australasian Catholic Record,* 86/4 (2009): 457–67.

Here I will explore a further idea found in Karl Rahner's theology. His understanding of Christian decision-making is based on an interpretation of Ignatius of Loyola's rules for the discernment of spirits. Ignatius's rules are sophisticated and subtle, but Rahner is convinced that one fundamental insight in these rules is highly significant for ordinary Christian life as well as for Christian theology.[4] Ignatius speaks of a God-given basis for discernment, when a person is drawn wholly to the love of God, in an experience of God's presence and love that comes as an inexplicable pure gift. It is not due to one's own perception or knowledge, nor the result of one's own acts of intellect and will.

Such an experience of consolation, of joy and peace in God, can be distinguished from more superficial experiences of consolation that may have their origin in ourselves, or in the movements pulling us in different directions, which Ignatius calls good and evil spirits. Ignatius calls the experience that is a sheer gift of God's grace a consolation 'without previous cause'.[5] In such an experience, he says, 'there can be no deception, since it proceeds from God alone'.[6] However, he points out that it is important to distinguish the original time of consolation from the time that follows, when our human reasoning, plans, and concepts, and the various pulls upon us of good and evil spirits, mean that we can well be deceived.

Rahner offers a contemporary reading of Ignatius's consolation without previous cause. Some scholars debate the accuracy of Rahner's interpretation of Ignatius, and some disagree with Rahner's theological positions.[7] I will not attempt to engage in these debates, but simply explore an application of Rahner's thought in the theology

---

4. See Karl Rahner's early work, 'The Logic of Concrete Individual Knowledge in Ignatius Loyola', in *The Dynamic Element in the Church* (London: Burns and Oats, 1964), 84–170. Rahner returns to this discussion in his *Ignatius of Loyola Speaks*, translated by Annemarie Kidder (South Bend, Ind: St Augustine's Press, 2013). For his application of these ideas to fundamental theology, see his 'Reflections on a New Task for Fundamental Theology', *Theological Investigations*, 16 (New York: Crossroad, 1979), 156–66.

5. Ignatius of Loyola, *The Spiritual Exercises*, in Louis J Puhl, editor and translator, *The Spiritual Exercises of St Ignatius: Based on Studies in the Language of the Autograph* (Chicago: Loyola University Press, 1951), paragraph 330, 147.

6. Ignatius, *The Spiritual Exercises*, paragraph 336, 149–50.

7. For a discussion of these controversies, see Philip Endean, *Karl Rahner and Ignatian Spirituality* (Oxford: Oxford University Press, 2001).

of receptive ecumenism. Fundamentally Rahner interprets the con-solation without cause as a human experience of God's Holy Spirit, against which we can test a proposed decision. In what follows I will first outline Rahner's position on the experience of the Spirit, and then his view of Christian decision-making, before briefly applying this line of thought to receptive ecumenism.

Rahner on the Experience of the Spirit

Can we really claim that we do experience the Spirit of God? The fact that all experience is mediated by language, culture and the psychol-ogy of the experiencer, suggests a critical and cautious approach to claims about the experience of the Holy Spirit. We know that pre-existing understandings and language always enter into experience and are necessary aspects of its interpretation. Experience is, by necessity, filtered through the psychological history and imaginative life of the individual subject. It is fundamental to note, as well, that for Rahner the experience of the Spirit is not of the same order as the experience of particular objects in the world, such as a tree, a dog or a human being. The experience of the Spirit is a far more obscure, mysterious, and global experience, one that occurs in and through these ordinary experiences of life.

Rahner insists that, although the experience of the Spirit of God is always an experience of incomprehensible mystery, it is something that does occur in ordinary human lives. In fact, the experience of God is a major theme in Rahner's theological work, and at the end of his life he insisted that all of his theology grew from the profound conviction at the heart of St. Ignatius's *Spiritual Exercises* that we really do experience the living God.[8]

Rahner is an advocate for what he called the 'mysticism of everyday life': not only the great saints, he insists, but also ordinary Christians are called to the mystical. In the light of increasing secularization, Rahner argues that in the future Christian faith will have to spring from interior conviction, and that it will need to involve personal experience of God. He expresses this in his saying that the Christian of the future will be a mystic, or he or she will be nothing.

---

8. Rahner, *Ignatius of Loyola Speaks*, 6–23.

Because he is convinced that ordinary people do experience the Spirit, but also that this can be an obscure and unnoticed experience, Rahner believes that the proclamation of the gospel of Jesus should begin from the place where the Spirit is already at work in a person's life, and is already experienced, at least in an obscure way. He sees it as fundamental for pastoral practice to evoke such experiences of the Spirit, to bring them to consciousness. He names the pastoral process of evoking where a person or a community experiences mystery and transcendence as the practice of mystagogy.

Rahner's understanding of the experience of the Spirit begins from his analysis of human knowing and loving of other creatures in the world. He shows that such everyday knowing and loving is always accompanied by an experience of mystery, whether it be consciously attended to or not. By mystery he means the experience of what is boundless and incomprehensible, beyond all our everyday concepts and language. Mystery points to the inexhaustible depths of the reality that we encounter in the everyday. In our knowing of another creature we form a concept of the specific person or object, and as we focus on the specific person or object, we always do this within a wider context or horizon. Although we do not always notice it, this wider context involves all other possible objects of knowledge. We situate specific objects of knowledge against an unlimited range of possible knowing. There is always an openness to more. When we ask questions, they open us up to further questions. Our minds are never satisfied. The horizon of our everyday knowing is boundless, reaching out towards the infinite.

We experience mystery not only in our knowing, but also in our loving. Particular acts of love for another can contain an implicit invitation to a love that is unconditioned and that has no boundaries. The partial fulfilment we experience in our love and commitment to others can open out towards a love that has no limits. There is a restless yearning that is not met, and which cannot be loaded onto the limited human objects of our love, without doing great damage. There is a boundless expanse to the human mind and heart, and this boundless expanse is always there as the context of ordinary knowledge and love.

In itself, such human experience is open to many interpretations. In the light of Christian revelation of the grace of God poured out in our world, Rahner understands these experiences as opening out to the love of the God of Jesus. He sees the grace of Christ as present in the Spirit to human beings of every time and place. Grace is then, the Spirit of God present in self-offering love, an offer that each person is free to accept or reject. Because of God's gracious presence to each person in the Spirit, the openness to mystery we experience can be understood as openness to the Spirit of Christ. The dynamic openness of the human person is Grace-filled, and Spirit-filled. In the light of revelation, the experience of mystery can then be known to be the experience of Grace, or the experience of the Spirit, or as Rahner often says, the experience of Holy Mystery.

Rahner proposes, as well, that there are special moments of Grace in our lives, where we are brought to a particular awareness of this Holy Mystery. In these circumstances, he suggests, the creaturely reality with which we are involved itself becomes a pointer to the Holy Mystery, so that the experience of the Spirit is brought to the forefront of consciousness. Rahner offers many examples of such experiences, many of them disquieting experiences, where the limits of the everyday break down, and we are led beyond ourselves into the incomprehensible mystery of God. He speaks of someone attempting to forgive, even when there is no reward for it, and the forgiveness is taken for granted; of someone trying to love God, even when there seems no obvious response; of someone who makes a decision to follow conscience even though this cannot be explained to others. In such moments, what at first seems like emptiness and darkness can be found to be the place where Love is with us, where we are held in Love. There are, of course, also overwhelmingly beautiful experiences, such as the birth of a child, or the sublime experience of the night sky, or a moment of prayer, that open out to mystery, to wonder, and to the God who fills all things.

Making Decisions on the Basis of the Experience of the Spirit

What Rahner sees as foundational for Christian decision-making is the experience of the Holy Spirit, a time, or times, in our lives when we are open to the mystery of the incomprehensible God, an experience of presence and love that is beyond all concepts and words. While the Holy Spirit is always present, there are particular times when we become open to and more aware of encountering the Spirit. While we interpret this encounter only through human images, concepts and words, these point beyond themselves towards the mystery that transcends them. Rahner sees such an experience of the Spirit as a touchstone for discernment in the ordinary circumstances of day-to-day life.

The process Rahner has in mind for Christian decision-making is a kind of prayerful thought experiment: 'The particular that is met with or that must be chosen, done, or undergone, is placed within this pure openness and receptivity of this consciously experienced transcendence, and kept there.'[9] The idea is to bring to conscious attention our deepest experience of God's grace along with the matter to be discerned. It is a matter of testing to see whether a potential decision 'sits' well with the place in our being where we are most open to God. Avery Dulles describes the process: 'Through a process of 'play acting' we imaginatively place ourselves in the situation we are on the point of choosing, attempting to measure whether it is translucent to pure consolation.'[10] Such testing may need to take place over a long time. In this process the choice we make is not directly revealed by God. We make the decision in the light of our perception of the 'fit' between the matter being discerned and our experience of God. Does the proposed course of action sit with our deepest experience of God in such a way as to produce a sense of peace in God?

As philosophers have clarified the systematic logical rules that govern human thinking, so Rahner sees Ignatius as offering a systematic approach to the logic of Christian decision-making. While he recognises that Ignatius builds on the ancient tradition of discernment, he sees Ignatius as offering 'the first and so far the only detailed method' for discerning the invitation of the Spirit in the concrete circumstances of everyday life.[11] The experience of grace, the experience of the Spirit, functions as a kind of first principle in the logic of Christian decision-making.

Just as an ordinary person uses logic without having studied it, Rahner argues, ordinary people often make important decisions more or less in the way suggested by Ignatius. A person might ponder something to be decided over some time, and then make a decision on the basis of what feels right and in harmony with her global sense

9. Rahner, 'The Logic of Concrete Individual Knowledge', 155–56.

10. Avery Dulles, 'The Ignatian Experience as Reflected in the Spiritual Theology of Karl Rahner', in *Jesuit Spirit in a Time of Change*, edited by Raymond Schroff (Westminster MD: Newman Press, 1968), 36.

11. Rahner, 'The Logic of Concrete Individual Knowledge', 115.

of herself. Theologically, Rahner points out, this global sense of herself may include her deepest sense of herself before God. This deepest sense of self is the place of grace, the place of the Holy Spirit.

Such a decision is made not only on the basis of rational analysis, but also by a sense of what 'suits' a person deep down. Many people express the need to 'sleep' on a decision. It seems that they need time to find out what is congruent with their true sense of self in a particular context. This true sense of self, of course, is not the place of self-absorption but the place of freedom and love, the place of letting go of self in the selflessness of love. In the light of this, Rahner suggests that faithful Christians 'who have never heard of St. Ignatius's instructions nevertheless instinctively make their decisions by their everyday religious logic in essentially the same way as Ignatius provides for'.[12]

We always face the danger of delusion: If I decide something on the basis that I feel 'at home' with it, this can easily be a self-centered judgment. It simply indicates that the proposal does not take me out of my comfort zone. The refined process suggested by Ignatius creates the possibility of finding freedom to make the hard choice. It seeks to ensure that I am testing a decision not against a superficial sense of myself, but against a real openness to the otherness of God.

Receptive Ecumenism: Discernment, Decision-Making and Reception

How might this process contribute to discernment, decision-making and reception of what is offered by a partner church? My proposal here is that there can be a parallel at the level of church to what Rahner proposes at the level of the individual. I offer an example from my own experience. If I as a Roman Catholic were to ask whether my church should more fully receive the institutional charism of synodality, offered to my church by the Orthodox, Anglican, and Lutheran partner churches, among others, then I might test this proposal, not only according to the criteria suggested at the beginning of this chapter, but also by bringing the idea of the reception of synodality to the deepest place of my personal experience of the Spirit, and testing it with this experience of the Spirit. This step, however, as important as it is, does not yet amount to a communal and fully ecclesial discernment.

---

12. Rahner, 'The Logic of Concrete Individual Knowledge', 166–7.

How might this process become more of an ecclesial event? One possibility that presents itself is the process of group discernment, where people gather into discernment groups, in which they are led into contemplative prayer, and engage in a process of listening to the Word of God, listening to the Spirit, and listening to each other. But something more is needed for fully ecclesial discernment. Perhaps what is needed as the basis for ecclesial testing, then, is not simply a personal event of the Spirit, but also a communal, ecclesial event of the Spirit.

As I take this example from my own tradition a little further, it is important to say that I am fully confident that similar examples of ecclesial experience of the Spirit could be adduced from other Christian traditions. As a Roman Catholic, my churchly experience of the Spirit is profoundly connected to a particular moment when the Holy Spirit of God was experienced by the church community to which I belong, in a life-giving and undeniable way, in the Second Vatican Council. Surely there is no clearer expression of the presence and action of the Holy Spirit in the recent history of the Roman Catholic Church. My proposal, then, is this: what is offered by a partner church, in this case the commitment to increased synodality, can be tested not only against the personal sense of the Spirit, but also against the ecclesial experience of the Spirit of God in and through the Second Vatican Council. This testing would need to occur at every part of church life, including the *sensus fidelium* of the whole people of God, the theological community, and the teaching office of the church.

What I am suggesting is not simply a rational testing of the reception of synodality against the formal teaching of the Second Vatican Council. The Spirit of God may be calling the Roman Catholic Church beyond what is already taught. It would be, rather, a testing of synodality for its congruence with the whole way in which the Holy Spirit was, and is, experienced in and through the Second Vatican Council. This is the Spirit who leads us back to the deepest aspects of the Christian tradition, the Spirit who invites us into a more faithful following of the way of Jesus, the Spirit who constantly leads the church into the new of God.

Bibliography

Dulles, Avery, 'The Ignatian Experience as Reflected in the Spiritual Theology of Karl Rahner', in *Jesuit Spirit in a Time of Change* edited by Raymond Schroff (Westminster MD: Newman Press, 1968), 23–41.

Edwards, Denis, 'Receptive Ecumenism and the Charism of a Partner Church: The Example of Justification', in *The Australasian Catholic Record* 86/4 (2009): 457–67.

Endean, Philip, *Karl Rahner and Ignatian Spirituality* (Oxford: Oxford University Press, 2001).

Ignatius of Loyola, *The Spiritual Exercises* in *The Spiritual Exercises of St. Ignatius: Based on Studies in the Language of the Autograph* edited and translated by Louis J Puhl (Chicago: Loyola University Press, 1951).

Orsy, Ladislas, 'Authentic Learning and Receiving—A Search for Criteria', in *Receptive Ecumenism and the Call to Catholic Learning*, edited by Paul D Murray (Oxford: Oxford University Press, 2008), 39–51.

Rahner, Karl, *Ignatius of Loyola Speaks*, translated by Annemarie Kidder (South Bend, Ind: St Augustine's Press, 2013).

Rahner, Karl, 'Reflections on a New Task for Fundamental Theology', *Theological Investigations,* 16 (New York: Crossroad, 1979), 156–66.

Rahner, Karl, 'The Logic of Concrete Individual Knowledge in Ignatius Loyola', in *The Dynamic Element in the Church* (London: Burns and Oats, 1964), 84–170.

Rusch, William G, *Ecumenical Reception: Its Challenge and Opportunity* (Grand Rapids, MI: Eerdmans, 2006).

Bernard Lonergan, Decision and Ecumenical Discernment

Karen Petersen Finch

'A firm foundation of friendship will enable us . . . to be open to sharing the discernment of a way forward that is faithful to the mind of
Christ pressed upon us as disciples.'[1] Justin Welby, Archbishop of
Canterbury, spoke these words to Pope Francis on June 14, 2013. His
words suggest that the term 'discernment' can serve as an expression
of hope in the presence of differences that may seem overwhelming.
It carries the echo of someone peering into the dark, looking for evidence of a 'way forward'—a trailhead that is not obvious to all but is
nevertheless real and promising.

Yet the same word also functions more ambiguously in ecumenical contexts. In their third report, members of the International
Reformed-Catholic Dialogue (IRCD—2007) defined 'discernment'
as the identification of God's will for a Christian community in its
unique time and place.[2] Our human discernment rests on the prompting of the Holy Spirit in the 'signs of the times,' in the biblical witness,
and in doctrine or tradition.[3] Yet separated churches may read these
sources differently and continue to do so until there is an entrenched
hermeneutical 'pattern of discernment'. The result may be stalemate,

---

1. 'Visit to Rome of His Grace Justin Welby, Archbishop of Canterbury (Meeting
   with Pope Francis, 14 June 2013)', *Information Service, Pontifical Council
   for Promoting Christian Unity,* 141/1 (2013): 11–12, at <http://www.vatican.
   va/roman_curia/pontifical_councils/chrstuni/information_service/pdf/
   information_service_141_en.pdf>. Accessed 11 April 2018.
2. World Alliance of Reformed Churches and Pontifical Council for Promoting
   Christian Unity, 'The Church as a Community of Common Witness to the
   Kingdom of God' (2007): 125–9, at <http://www.prounione.urbe.it/dia-int/r-rc/
   doc/e_r-rc_3-contents.html>. Accessed 21 April 2018.
3. 'Community of Common Witness', 140–1.

accompanied by a longing that through continued relationship 'our different patterns of discernment may begin to converge'.[4]

Based on these and many other examples, I would argue that discernment, as the term is used in ecumenical literature, refers to a blend of both objective and subjective knowing. To 'discern' is to see what is really there, what the Holy Spirit is really up to, even if it might be hard to spot. The IRCD report gives discernment this objective sense when it notes how difficult it can be to 'discover the true nature of particular situations, their causes or solutions'.[5] There must, however, be a subjective angle to discernment if different ecumenical partners can look at the same phenomena and 'read' them in totally different ways. Moreover, the way it is commonly presented, ecumenical discernment appears to go beyond knowledge and to include an element of decision. As Archbishop Welby put it, we must be 'open to sharing the discernment of a way forward'. We can *choose* to live within a 'pattern of discernment' (IRCD) that is habitual and comfortable, or we can *choose* to look through a lens—the lens of the dialogue partner—and 'see' a different picture. Common usage suggests that ecumenical discernment depends on the will as well as on our powers of perception.

Clearly 'discernment' is shorthand for a plethora of epistemological issues. Do our decisions and desires play a role in what we perceive? Is there a real way forward, a set of discoverable truths on which we can agree and rely? What if those truths exist, but we perceive them differently? We cannot tackle all these issues at once, but there is a fruitful approach available to us in the idea that discernment includes an element of decision. Fr Bernard Lonergan, a Jesuit theologian and philosopher who died in 1984, has explored the role of decision within the formation of knowledge at great depth. In daily life, we tend to assume that decision is a step after knowing: first we know, and then we decide or do. Yet Lonergan viewed decision as a component of knowing itself. This unusual way of speaking about knowing may be useful to those who recognise the complex nature of ecumenical discernment, which appears to have existential, objective *and* subjective dimensions.

---

4. 'Community of Common Witness', 147.
5. 'Community of Common Witness', 129.

This article has three goals. First, we will clarify how knowledge and decision are related within Lonergan's cognitional theory. In other words, we will probe what Lonergan had to say about the existential aspect of discernment. Secondly, we will move from Lonergan's general method—which describes human knowing—to his special method, which describes theological inquiry in particular. Lonergan's method supports our attentiveness to the existential aspect of discernment while we are doing theology, and especially ecumenical theology. Finally, we will end with reflection on the nature of ecumenical discernment as both objective and subjective, informed by Lonergan's thinking. The common-sense epistemologies of our day tend to suggest that we must choose between one or the other. Perhaps they are also driving the classic dichotomy between the 'ecumenism of truth' (Faith and Order) and the 'ecumenism of life' (Life and Work).[6] Yet Christians cannot be meaningfully divided in two: a brain for doctrine and a heart, or a will, for relationships and witness. More unitive epistemological approaches are needed to help us discern 'a way forward that is faithful to the mind of Christ'.

Decision is Part of Knowing: Lonergan's Cognitional Theory

Bernard Lonergan's influence is located at the intersection of theology, epistemology and ethics: a fitting location for talking about discernment. He believed that solid practice in all three areas requires that we 'thoroughly understand what it is to understand'.[7] Surprisingly for a theologian, Lonergan began with empirical observation of what our minds are doing when we are pursuing knowledge. To clarify the role that decision plays in knowledge, we need to start with what he called the structure of cognition.

Lonergan identified four cognitive 'operations' that flow naturally into one another: experience, understanding, judgment and decision.[8] These innate habits of mind work together to move a person

---

6. 'Community of Common Witness', 3.
7. Bernard Lonergan, *Insight: A Study of Human Understanding*, edited by Frederick Crowe and Robert Doran (Toronto: University of Toronto Press, 1992), 22.
8. Bernard Lonergan, 'Philosophical Positions with Regard to Knowing', in *Philosophical and Theological Papers 1958-1964*, edited by Robert Croken, Frederick Crowe, and Robert Doran (Toronto: University of Toronto Press, 1996), 215.

toward reliable knowledge. The key fact about the operations is that none of them, on its own, constitutes knowing. At the level of experience, one is paying attention to the data that is given to one's senses. But sense perception is not enough, because the human world is also full of meanings that are truly and powerfully present but cannot be touched or seen. Meaning is discerned by means of questions. Think of the two-year-old who asks, 'Why? Why?'[9] The answer to the 'why' question does not just 'come into the eyeballs' of the toddler, because as Lonergan famously said, knowing is not just 'gaping' or taking a look.[10] Rational humans will inevitably ask questions about the sense data they apprehend.

Questions like 'What is it?' or 'How does it work?' bring us naturally to employ the second operation: understanding or insight.[11] To illustrate the role of insight, I ask the science students in my theology courses to identify where a hypothesis comes from. They quickly realise that a hypothesis is not given in data; it is an achievement of mind. In the middle of scientific method there is an element that is not reducible to sense experience, which is very surprising to students who have been nurtured on strong empiricism. In fact, discernment seeks the intelligible in the sensible: we ask, 'What does it mean?' and we answer with proposals, with hypotheses and explanations.

It is helpful here to pause and identify the source of this dynamism of cognition. Why does experience move us to ask questions of meaning, questions that cannot be answered by simply referring to sense experience in a never-ending loop? ('It is what it is what it is . . . ') Lonergan was working in the tradition of Thomas Aquinas and believed that humans are born with an 'unrestricted desire to know'. From a Thomist perspective, God would not have given us an unrestricted desire for meaning without also providing its satisfaction. We desire not only meaning, but true meaning that is 'independent of us and our thinking'.[12] Its only real satisfaction is God himself, who is meaning overflowing. Therefore, the unrestricted desire to know is really an unrestricted desire for God. It is inherently theological and even moral, for the possibility of falsehood is all around us. We live

---

9. Joseph Fitzpatrick, *Philosophical Encounters: Lonergan and the Analytical Tradition* (Toronto: University of Toronto Press, 2005), 3.

10. Lonergan, 'Philosophical Positions with Regard to Knowing', 215.

11. Lonergan, *Insight*, 308.

12. Bernard Lonergan, *Method in Theology* (Toronto: University of Toronto Press, 1971), 35.

among meanings that must always be tested because 'meaning can go astray, because there is myth as well as science, fiction as well as fact, deceit as well as honesty, error as well as truth'.[13] Hence the need for discernment, in ecumenical settings as well as in other arenas of life.

The need to test every insight leads to the third spontaneous operation of cognition which Lonergan called judgment. Human beings do not only value discernment—we value *right* discernment. Insight proposes a meaningful explanation of what is given to our experience, but it does not guarantee that our explanation is correct. As Lonergan wryly observed, 'insights are a dime a dozen and most of them are wrong'.[14] We naturally desire insights that will stand up to scrutiny and serve as a solid ground for living. Am I or am I not discerning what is really so? This question represents the cognitional operation of judgment which Lonergan believed is inevitable for us. It belies the popular idea that there can be knowledge without judgment. The person who tells you that 'there is no absolute truth' has made a judgment about the nature of truth and is asking you to make a judgment about their judgment. In a backhanded way, he or she is providing evidence for our everyday working assumption that it is possible to know the world in an objective way. We will return to Lonergan's views on objectivity at the end of this article.

Paradoxically, when Lonergan introduced judgment into his cognitional theory, he was not only testifying to the possibility and importance of objective knowing; at the same time, he was celebrating the subjective element as well. One can say that judgment is the ownership of knowledge, in which we provide personal assent or dissent within the process of discernment. This is why, for Lonergan, knowing is not rightly conceived on the analogy of passive sense perception. We look, but we also understand and judge, and in judgment the existential element of discernment is implicit. It became explicit when Lonergan named the fourth cognitional operation as 'decision,' indicating that he was drawing not only on the Thomist tradition but also on modernity's exploration of human intentionality. In other words, decision refers to the persons we are becoming as we are discerning. Especially through our judgments of fact and value, we make of ourselves a new kind of fact, or a new kind of value.

---

13. Lonergan, *Method in Theology,* 77. Lonergan was aware that this use of the word myth is pejorative and 'out of line with current usage'.
14. Lonergan, 'Philosophical Positions with Regard to Knowing,' 217.

Sometimes new knowledge is so transformative that we find our worldview is too confining and its parameters must be totally redrawn. Lonergan called this conversion: a kind of seismic learning that happens at the level of decision.[15] Intellectual conversion occurs when we decide to leave behind the myth that knowing is like taking a look. Moral conversion is a movement of the will toward 'opting for the truly good, even for value against satisfaction when value and satisfaction conflict'.[16] Religious conversion is the grace-enabled transformation of our entire lives because we have 'fallen in love with God'.[17] To be open to continual transformation in all three of these existential dimensions, is to be what Lonergan called an 'authentic' person.[18] Such a person brings a converted subjectivity to the acts of experiencing, understanding, judging and deciding, increasing the likelihood of wise—even objective—discernment.

What are the implications for ecumenical discernment if we consider, along with Lonergan, that decision is a part of knowing? Three come to mind. First, the quality of our ecumenical decisions will depend on the authenticity of our knowing in the other three operations. A decision is not just a leap into the dark. We have the opportunity and the responsibility to be attentive to data, intelligent in grasping meaning, and reasonable in judgment. All of this is playing a role in what we typically call 'discernment'. If we are attentive to knowing, and to decision as an aspect of it, we can get better and better at both.

Second, our contemporary intellectual climate encourages the assumption that judgment and dialogue are mutually exclusive; by making judgments, I am forcing them on other people and I risk breaking the dialogue 'container'. But we are all making judgments, all the time, and we should be. The difference is that dialogue participants can learn to voice their judgments honestly and to hold them lightly, knowing them to be revisable. The most important decision that we make in dialogue is the decision to learn, which includes revising our judgments as well as seeking new experience and insights. From the standpoint of this decision, even deep differences of judgment become opportunities for ecumenical discernment and conversion.

---

15. Lonergan, *Method in Theology*, 240.
16. Lonergan, *Method in Theology*, 240.
17. Lonergan, *Method in Theology*, 240.
18. Lonergan, *Method in Theology*, 240.

Third, Lonergan's model suggests that there is no hard and fast distinction between human beings as theoretical thinkers and human beings as practical decision-makers. What happens to the traditional distinction between Faith and Order/Life and Work if we acknowledge that decisions are happening in both contexts? Instead of false dichotomies, we need a theological method that supports good decision-making, and therefore good discernment, in all forms of ecumenical engagement. That is the focus of the next section.

Method and Ecumenical Discernment

If Lonergan was right, perhaps the biggest benefit of a recurrent cognitional structure is the ability to discern it happening in oneself, which he called self-appropriation.[19] If I can understand what it is to understand, I can supercharge my ability to discern, because I am sharpening my intellectual tools even while I am using them. For this reason, Lonergan wondered if there might be a benefit to conceiving a specific method for theology that recapitulated the structure of cognition. He reasoned that theology is also a dynamic unity of inter-related activities: interpreting scripture, historical analysis, etc. He also knew that the goals of each cognitional operation—'be attentive, be intelligent, be reasonable, be responsible'—are certainly appropriate goals for theologians.[20] Above all, method makes us conscious to ourselves, creating awareness of 'what we are doing when we are doing theology' so that we may perform those activities more effectively, and with greater authenticity. These and other reflections became the foundation of Lonergan's 1971 book entitled *Method in Theology*.

The following chart indicates how Lonergan recast his cognitional theory into a framework for theological discernment. Given that our current focus is the existential aspect of discernment, it makes sense to pay attention to the two activities that Lonergan particularly associated with the cognitional operation of decision. In everyday life our decisions mediate between the realities of the past and the possibilities of the future. In this method, *dialectic* and *foundations* form the turning point between the first phase of Lonergan's method (in which theologians receive the past) and the second phase (in which they shape the church's future).

---

19. Lonergan, *Method in Theology*, 7, 17.
20. Lonergan, *Method in Theology*, 231.

Theological Task	Associated with:
FIRST PHASE: Reception* Research (clarifying the field of data)	Experience
Interpretation (of scripture and tradition)	Understanding
History (ideas in their contexts)	Judgment
Dialectic (the roots of difference)	**Decision**
SECOND PHASE: Proclamation* **Foundations (conversion and difference)**	**Decision**
Doctrines (what we have learned)	Judgment
Systematics (how doctrines interelate)	Understanding
Communications (how theology passes to the Church)	Experience
*my terms	

Lonergan incorporated these two activities into his method to emphasise that theology is never monolithic or personally neutral. Firstly, *dialectic* equips us to cope with diversity within theology and to discern the various causes of theological difference.[21] Theologians have always selected the field of data on which their inquiries would focus (*research*); they have wrestled with the *interpretation* of Scripture and tradition; and they have put forth narratives and judgments about the meaning of *history* and their place in it. These are all aspects of theological discernment, and ecumenists know that results can vary widely. Some differences are merely perspectival (due to time and place and circumstance). But others stem from decisions which, once they are made, take on the patina of unquestionable authority.

An example from my own tradition is the wholesale rejection of natural theology. Many Reformed theologians have decided to condemn natural theology as synonymous with the exercise of autonomous human reason. Elsewhere I have argued against this decision.[22] I believe that it rests on inadequate interpretations of Scripture, of John Calvin, and of Thomas Aquinas. It has been reinforced by a history of polemic and mutual misunderstanding. It tends to involve

---

21. Lonergan, *Method in Theology,* 231.
22. Karen Petersen Finch, 'The Reformed Rejection of Natural Theology: Dialectic and Foundations', in *METHOD: Journal of Lonergan Studies*, 6/2 (2015): 19–34.

theologians in the performative contradiction of using reason to argue that we cannot know God through reason. In short, the rejection of natural theology is a decision which, having once been made by human beings, can also be unmade. By asking what role decision has played in the formation of our respective traditions, dialectic makes new discernment possible into seemingly intransigent topics such as the relationship between nature and grace, between the *analogia entis* and the *analogia fidei*.[23]

Foundations is a neologism that means 'reflection on conversion'.[24] Conversion, of course, is existential; it is 'a fundamental and momentous change in the human reality that a theologian is'.[25] It is the most important decision in human life and it is not of human origin. Lonergan placed foundations at the center of his theological method out of a belief that the threefold conversion 'lights up' our discernment both in earthly matters and in theological inquiry. And Lonergan did not see a hard and fast line between religious conversion, which is transforming grace, and intellectual or moral conversion. In ecumenical dialogue especially, it is dangerous to separate the three. We are drawn into ecumenical relationships by our common baptism, the origin of which is God's love poured out into our hearts by grace and faith (Rom 5:5). That is what Lonergan meant by religious conversion. But dialogue is a form of learning, and learning is a form of knowing, and knowing together requires epistemological sensitivity lest possible achievements on the doctrinal or missional level become undone by entrenched habits on the epistemological level. This is intellectual conversion: being attentive to what we are doing when we are knowing.

Finally, without continual moral conversion, no one will have the courage to ask the hard questions that permeate ecumenical practice. We can think of foundations as dialectic turned inward, with conversion as the litmus test. It is easy enough to look at the theology of the past and to judge that the Reformed rejection of natural theology is

---

23. For example, many theologians approach the possibility of an *analogia entis* as a doctrinal question, without having observed that it is also an epistemological question. Both Protestants and Catholics are using the word 'analogy' as a word picture that stands for their preferred epistemological posture. Dialectic is greatly needed.

24. Lonergan, *Method in Theology*, 131.

25. Lonergan, *Method in Theology*, 270.

not sufficiently rooted in intellectual, moral or religious conversion. It is much more difficult to look at my own theology of the present and ask the relevant personal questions. Have I brought a converted self to this article as I am writing it? Do I write and teach and dialogue as someone who has fallen in love with God? Am I intellectually consistent and courageous? Do I demonstrate godly love toward my colleagues in other traditions?

If the good news of dialectic is that decisions can change, the good news of foundations is that theologians can change. That is why Lonergan located foundations at the center of his theological method and associated it with the self-constituting act of decision.

Conclusion: Discernment is Objective and Subjective

We began this article by acknowledging that the word 'discernment' occurs frequently in ecumenical discourse, but in a way that is complex. A focus on decision enabled us to pull the existential thread of the tangle and see where that took us, informed by the theology of Bernard Lonergan. While focusing on decision, we were honoring the so-called 'subjective' aspects of knowing. Human beings do not come passively or neutrally to the task of learning or knowledge-formation or discernment, whatever language one chooses to use. It is important to find a theological method that supports the existential and subjective aspects of knowing so that we are more and more aware of how we are constituting ourselves, and our communities, in the very act of discernment.

Yet discernment in common parlance also reflects a concern for objectivity, for seeing reality as it is, independently of what we may want it to be. The great strength of Lonergan's work is that he did not drive a wedge between objectivity and subjectivity as many twentieth-century philosophers and theologians have done. Those who are philosophically minded, and want to study Lonergan in more depth, should note that he was a realist; he did believe in a real universe that we are able to know. But he was a critical realist, and the word 'critical' refers in particular to knowledge through judgment. For Lonergan it is possible to test our beliefs and see how close they are to reality, and this testing kind of discernment involves not just empirical knowing but the whole person. Thus objectivity becomes 'the fruit of authentic subjectivity,' of attending to the four operations and following bravely where they lead.[26]

Bibliography

Fitzpatrick, Joseph, *Philosophical Encounters: Lonergan and the Analytical Tradition* (Toronto: University of Toronto Press, 2005).

Lonergan, Bernard, *Insight: A Study of Human Understanding*, edited by Frederick Crowe and Robert Doran (Toronto: University of Toronto Press, 1992).

Lonergan, Bernard, 'Insight Revisited', in *A Second Collection*, edited by William Ryan and Bernard Tyrrell (Toronto: University of Toronto Press, 1996), 263–78.

Lonergan, Bernard, *Method in Theology* (Toronto: University of Toronto Press, 1971).

Lonergan, Bernard, 'Philosophical Positions with Regard to Knowing', in *Philosophical and Theological Papers* 1958-1964, edited by Robert Croken, Frederick Crowe, and Robert Doran (Toronto: University of Toronto Press, 1996), 214–43.

Murray, Paul, 'Introducing Receptive Ecumenism', in *The Ecumenist: A Journal of Theology, Culture and Society*, 51/ 2 (2014): 1–9.

Petersen Finch, Karen, 'The Reformed Rejection of Natural Theology: Dialectic and Foundations', in METHOD: *Journal of Lonergan Studies*, 6/2 (2015): 19–34.

'Visit to Rome of His Grace Justin Welby, Archbishop of Canterbury (Meeting with Pope Francis, 14 June 2013)', in *Information Service, Pontifical Council for Promoting Christian Unity*, 141/1 (2013): 11–12. at <http://www.vatican.va/roman_curia/pontifical_councils/chrstuni/information_service/pdf/information_service_141_en.pdf>. Accessed 11 April 2018.

World Alliance of Reformed Churches and Pontifical Council for Promoting Christian Unity. 'The Church as a Community of Common Witness to the Kingdom of God' (2007). at <http://www.prounione.urbe.it/dia-int/r-rc/doc/e_r-rc_3-contents.html>. Accessed 21 April 2018.

---

26. P McShane, 'An Interview with Father Bernard Lonergan, S.J.', in *A Second Collection*, edited by William Ryan and Bernard Tyrrell (Toronto: University of Toronto Press, 1996), 214.

A Forum for Theology in the World Vol 5 No 2/2018

The Holy Spirit and Communion, Shaping Receptive Ecumenism

Elizabeth Welch

Introduction

The theme of the Holy Spirit and communion is key to an understanding of the underlying theological nature of Receptive Ecumenism. This theme sees communion as a gift of the one triune God, rooted in a dependency on the Holy Spirit. Receptive Ecumenism is about identifying the Spirit's presence at work in each other and, through that identification, being led by the Spirit towards the communion which is God's gift. This paper refers to the interweaving of different levels of communion from the personal to the universal, and includes a discussion of one particular contemporary ecumenical dialogue, namely the International Reformed Anglican Dialogue, which began in 2015 between the Anglican Communion and the World Communion of Reformed Churches. This Dialogue is referred to in order to look at the way in which Receptive Ecumenism, even if not named as such in the dialogue discussions, is at work in terms of the openness to receive different understandings of communion and to open the possibility of this reception helping these two communions to grow more closely together.

Receptive Ecumenism has rightly drawn attention to some of the difficult issues with regard to late twentieth and early twenty-first century approaches to ecumenism. The search for Christian self-identity has at times been stronger than a search for a shared identity in Christ, and has led to a re-enforcement of separated churches, rather than a growing together of different churches.

Setting the scene

The theme for the 1991 World Council of Churches Assembly, the theme was 'Come Holy Spirit, Renew the Whole Creation'. I was privileged to be present at this Assembly and can clearly remember the controversy, from the opening part of the Assembly, that arose because of two completely different presentations on the Spirit. The first was from Professor Chung Hyun Kyung from the Presbyterian Church in Korea, set in a visual context incorporating song and dance and raising the issue of 'spirits' as well as the Holy Spirit. The second was a formal Orthodox presentation, from a closely-read script on the Holy Spirit, rooted in the tradition of the Church going back to the early Fathers. Reflection on the Spirit became one of the contested issues at the Assembly and in the reporting and discussion that followed on from the Assembly. The discussion about the Holy Spirit included looking at the nature of the Holy Spirit within the Christian tradition alongside the question about the presence of the Spirit in different religions, as well as how to identify the work of the *Holy* Spirit as over against a more general view of spirits. I remember the intense discussion in a Faith and Order working group, on the nature of legitimate diversity, in the midst of the range of views in this and other areas of understanding of the faith.

At this Assembly, in the discussion of the Holy Spirit, the emphasis was more on articulating the range of views held in different churches than being open to receiving the Holy Spirit as interpreted by a different tradition. Receptive Ecumenism points to the need for a willingness to be open to receive from others, as well as to be able to speak from the point of self-identity. The Canberra example points to the time it takes, beginning with a different tradition articulating their own understanding of the Holy Spirit, to being open to receive a different understanding of the Holy Spirit from another tradition of the church. Receptive Ecumenism, with its emphasis on receiving from each other, helps to focus on moving on from separated identities to seeing a shared identity in the power of the Spirit.

Discussions about the nature and role of the Holy Spirit have expanded since the early days of the twentieth century, initially with the rise of Pentecostalism and the charismatic movement, and then more recently, in the past half-century, in extensive writing about the

Holy Spirit.[1] This writing has in part been allied to the re-emphasis of the significance of Trinitarian thinking for the Christian faith. Ever since the early councils of the church, there have been discussions about how to understand the nature of the Trinity. One of the more recent contemporary issues is the understanding of the 'three-in-one, one-in-three' dimensions of the three persons in the Christian understanding of God. A renewed emphasis on the Trinity at the heart of the Christian faith has led to a revived focus on the nature of communion. This has included a discussion on the significance of personal relationality, both within the Trinity and flowing out to embrace people and creation. Key to an understanding of the triune God is a focus on the communion within the Holy Trinity, a communion into which people and creation are drawn through the life, death and resurrection of Jesus Christ and the power of the Holy Spirit, for the sake of the world.[2]

This understanding of communion has been under pressure, particularly in the west, from a range of factors. The Enlightenment focus on the individual has mitigated against an emphasis on the rela-

---

1. A small number of examples of writings on the large range of perspectives on the Holy Spirit from the second half of the twentieth century onwards include: *The Church in the Movement of the Spirit*, edited by William R Barr and Rena M Yocom (Grand Rapids, MI: Eerdmans, 1994); Hendrikus Berkhof, *The Doctrine of the Holy Spirit* (Richmond, VA: Westminster John Knox Press, 1986); James Joyce Buckley and David S Yeago, *Knowing the Triune God: the work of the Spirit in the Practices of the Church* (Grand Rapids, MI: Eerdmans, 2001); Yves Congar, *I Believe in the Holy Spirit* (London: Geoffrey Chapman, 1983); Gordon D Fee, *The Holy Spirit in the Letters of Paul* (Peabody, MA: Hendrickson, 1994); Andrew K Gabriel, *The Lord is the Spirit: The Holy Spirit and the Divine Attributes* (Cambridge: James Clarke & Co, 2012); George S Hendry, *The Holy Spirit in Christian Theology* (London: SCM, 1964); Alasdair Heron, *The Holy Spirit* (London: Marshall, Morgan and Scott, 1983); Robert Jensen, *The Triune Identity* (Philadelphia PA: Fortress Press, 1982); Veli-Matti Kärkkäinen, *Pneumatology: the Holy Spirit in Ecumenical, International, and Contextual Perspective* (Grand Rapids, MI: Baker Academic, 2002); John McIntyre, *The Shape of Pneumatology* (London: T & T Clark International, 2004); CFD Moule, *The Holy Spirit* (London: Mowbray, 1978); Ben Quash, *Found Theology: History, Imagination and the Holy Spirit* (London: Bloomsbury, 2013); EF Rogers, *After the Spirit: a Constructive Pneumatology from Resources Outside the Modern West* (London: SCM, 2006); Michael Welker, *God the Spirit* (Eugene, OR: Wipf and Stock 2013).
2. Catherine Mowry Lacugna, *God for us, the Trinity and Christian Life* (New York: HarperCollins 1991), 1, points to the way in which the Doctrine of the Trinity 'is ultimately a practical doctrine with radical consequences for Christian Life'.

tionality that comes out of participation in God's gift of communion. In this Enlightenment understanding, there has been a priority of emphasis on the individual in isolation, with the ability to determine for herself the needs, priorities and issues of her life, and a diminishing emphasis on the importance of life in community. This sense of self-determination has been accompanied by a rise of secularisation, as the understanding of a significant relationship with God has diminished. The role of faith in society is also no longer so clear. For example, in the United Kingdom there has been, on the one hand, a gradual lessening of church-going, and, on the other hand, a rise of an increasingly non-theistic orientation. This is seen demonstrated in rhetoric which at times points at justified challenges to the church and at other times points to a desire for a religion-free society.

It is perhaps not surprising that under these pressures, churches in the United Kingdom have felt the need to focus on their own self-identity rather than on the development of ecumenical relationships. Against this backdrop, one encouraging factor has been the rise of shared mission activity, such as foodbanks, engaging with refugees, and providing hospitality to the homeless. But the ecumenical activity has not necessarily been matched with in-depth ecumenical reflection on the nature of our separated Christian identities in our different churches and the way in which churches can nevertheless have a sense of their oneness in Christ, through the presence of the Holy Spirit.

The nature of Communion

'Communion' is a multi-dimensional word, weaving together the personal and the universal, and having implications for persons in relationship in a local community, as well as for the nature of relationships in national and international bodies of the church. What is significant is that communion starts by being the gift of the one triune God, who draws people and creation into the fullness of life, through the power of the Holy Spirit.[3]

---

3. An analysis of the nature of communion can be found in John Zizioulas, *Being as Communion* (London: Darton, Longman & Todd Ltd, 2004) and in Patricia A Fox, *God as Communion: John Zizioulas, Elizabeth Johnson, and the retrieval of the Symbol of the Triune God* (Collegeville, MN: Liturgical Press, 2001).

Communion is not only a universal and an international idea. Communion is embodied in each place in the sacrament of Holy Communion. This sacrament makes visible the death and resurrection of Jesus Christ through the invocation of the Holy Spirit. The personal reception of the bread and the wine points to the participation of each person in the body of Christ. But this understanding takes us to a place of wider ecumenical separation, in our inability to receive communion from one another, particularly between Protestant, Catholic and Orthodox traditions. The Orthodox theologian, Alexander Schmemann, points to 'the endless controversies which little by little transformed them [the bread and wine] into elements of an almost abstract theological speculation.'[4] He could have added 'and separation' as the interpretations of Holy Communion, both about the bread and the wine, and also about the way communion relates to the whole church, and the questions of who presides and who can receive, are still a potent reminder of our separated church life.

The nature of communion is that it is not an abstract idea, nor a remote doctrine, nor only a description of an international body of the church. Communion involves the person and the place. It is embodied in the everyday life of the church, through the activity of the Holy Spirit.

Between the personal and the universal lie the regional, the national and the international possibilities of the embodiment of communion. In each level of embodiment, it is important to look to the way in which it is the Holy Spirit who plays a key transformative role in bringing communion into being.

Communion and the Holy Spirit

Over the past century, from the wide-ranging discussion and reflection on the nature and activity of the Holy Spirit, three areas of thinking have emerged that are significant in terms of communion.

First, there is the transformative role of the Holy Spirit in bringing communion, in its broadest sense of the relationality that is possible with God, into being. This comes as a reminder of the significance of communion as God's gift, rather than, for example, as brought about

---

4. Alexander Schmemann *For the Life of the World* (Crestwood NY: St Vladimir's Seminary Press 1973), 33

by the good organisational ability of a human community. As with any gift, it is offered to be freely received, rather than having a sense of being enforced. The Spirit comes with power, but this is a power that points to diversity, as in, for example, the possibility of the Spirit being either like a mighty wind or a gentle breeze.[5] With this gift, there are many ways of receiving it. The Spirit comes as a reminder of both the presence of God and of the otherness of God. It is not possible to pin the Spirit down, or to claim the Spirit as the exclusive property of any one individual or church.

Second, the Spirit draws God's people into a communion that is embodied in prayer and worship. The moments of encounter with God are many-facetted. But above all else, it is in prayer and worship that people are drawn closer to the one triune God, to one another and, therefore, to participation in God's purpose for God's world. This then brings us to the complex area in which churches can be particularly challenged—the celebration of the sacrament of Holy Communion, an area which needs further work and development. The 2008 conference 'The Spirit in Worship, Worship in the Spirit' produced a helpful range of papers examining the variety of issues that arise when looking at the Spirit in Worship.[6]

If Receptive Ecumenism is about recognising and welcoming the presence of the Spirit in the different traditions of the church, there are further studies to be undertaken about the different understandings of the nature of prayer, spirituality and worship in and between the separated churches, in order to see how we can mutually recognise and welcome the gift of the Spirit in the variety of offerings that are possible.

Third, there is an eschatological dimension to the Spirit, as alluded to, for example, through Romans 8. Paul writes of the role of the Spirit in the Christian life, including references in verse 18 to the glory about to be revealed and in verse 23 to the contrast between receiving the first fruits of the Spirit and waiting for those first fruits to be fully

---

5. See, for example, the analysis of the different biblical ways in which the Spirit is encountered in Anthony C Thiselton, *The Holy Spirit: in Biblical Teaching, through the Centuries and Today* (Grand Rapids, MI: Eerdmans, 2013). Thiselton then places this biblical analysis into helpful contexts, both from perspectives across the centuries and in contemporary writing.

6. *The Spirit in Worship, Worship in the Spirit*, edited by Teresa Berger and Bryan D Spinks (Collegeville, MN: Liturgical Press, 2009).

realised. Paul comes with a reminder in verse 24 of the need to wait in hope for what is unseen and yet is to come. The Spirit does not only come from the past, but comes to us from the future, drawing us into God's future. This gives a two-fold dimension to looking at communion. We look at the past in terms of the way in which Spirit has been present with the churches across the centuries to shape the life of the church and we wrestle with the question of how the same Spirit might have led churches in different directions at different times. We also look to the future, to see the way in which that same Spirit is leading the church on into new ways of embodying God's life, and into new understandings of the truth of the Gospel.

The relationality into which we are drawn by our participation in the communion of the Holy Trinity inevitably opens up the imperative for relationality between separated churches. This relationality is not just something for which we work. It is on offer as the gift of the Holy Spirit, which we are invited to receive.

The Holy Spirit and Communion in International Dialogues

Another encouraging sign for the life of Receptive Ecumenism has been the range of ecumenical dialogues, both at national and international levels. Ecumenical dialogues indicate a first step on the road to Receptive Ecumenism, with a willingness of separated traditions to come together and reflect and pray together both on their differences and on the way in which God might be drawing them closer together. It is interesting to note those dialogues which have taken on communion as a positive theme to be explored in looking at the nature of shared working and co-operation. Jeremy Bergen has written a helpful article analysing the international bilateral dialogues from 1982 to 2012, with particular reference to the role of the Holy Spirit and communion.[7]

We now turn to a consideration of one particular international dialogue. The International Reformed Anglican Dialogue, which began in 2015, has, at the time of writing, met three times and is aiming to prepare a report on the theme of communion for its 2019

---

7. Jeremy M Bergen, 'The Holy Spirit and Lived Communion from the Perspective of International Bilateral Dialogues', in *Journal of Ecumenical Studies*, 49/2 (2014): 193–217.

meeting.[8] While Receptive Ecumenism as a phrase has not been actively pointed to, the nature of the dialogue, in the exploration of both differences and what might be learnt from one another is a pointer to the helpfulness of this way of thinking.

Dialogue between the two communions had previously culminated in 1984 with the publication of *God's Reign and our Unity*, a report which gave a renewed focus on mission. However, for a range of reasons, the dialogue did not start again until 2015, leaving a gap of just over thirty years. The theme of the present dialogue is Communion, a theme that has been already been taken up in a number of previous international dialogues.

What is the nature of Communion in terms of this Dialogue? This question is particularly pertinent in view of the formation of the World Communion of Reformed Churches in June 2010. This brought together the larger World Alliance of Reformed Churches and the smaller Reformed Ecumenical Council to form the largest international body for Reformed Christians, bringing together 233 churches from 110 countries and embracing, at some estimates, around 100 million people.

One of the discussions in the Dialogue has been about the way in which the Anglican Communion has a long tradition of understanding of the nature of communion, in view of its extensive experience of being a communion, dating back, it is thought, to 1847.[9] However, the Reformed Communion, in view of its newness, is still working through what communion means at this level of discourse. This comparison has provided a fruitful backdrop to the Dialogue, in terms of the shared exploration of these different understandings, which will now be outlined.

More work has been carried forward on the particular outworking of the nature of communion at the international level in the Anglican tradition, as is seen in the 2015 Working Paper *Towards a Symphony of Instruments*. This paper analyses both the ecclesiology of commu-

---

8. The writer of this paper has the privilege of being one of the co-chairs of this dialogue.

9. Quoting the writings of Avis and Podmore in *Towards a Symphony of Instruments, A Historical and Theological Consideration of the Instruments of Communion of the Anglican Communion*, a working paper prepared by the Inter-Anglican Standing Commission on Unity, Faith and Order (2015), 19, footnote 22.

nion and the nature of its embodiment, in the Lambeth Conference, the Ministry of the Archbishop of Canterbury, the Primates' Meeting, and the Anglican Consultative Council. The Paper concludes by looking at the way in which the Instruments are there for the mission of the church and are the gift of the Spirit.

Among the Reformed churches, the work on communion has been taken forward in a consultation in 2014, but is in a much earlier stage than that of the Anglican Communion, in terms of developing an understanding of 'Instruments of Communion'. Reformed churches tend to have a greater sense of their separate national identity and a lesser sense of their mutual international belonging than the churches of the Anglican Communion.

The conversations have looked at such areas as the balance between the desire for unity and the acknowledgement of legitimate diversity, the way in which different histories have shaped communions differently and the question of the nature of the work of the Holy Spirit in this different shaping. They have also discussed the key role of mutual hospitality, even in the midst of diversity.

In the Reformed-Anglican Dialogue discussions, it has been noted that the understanding of communion varies both between the different traditions and within each tradition. For neither Anglican nor Reformed traditions does it mean that we come with a united sense of what communion is within our own tradition. It has been noted that there are issues, such as human sexuality, which have tested the limits and boundaries of communion within each communion, and have raised the question as to which issues have the capability of being 'communion-breaking'.

In terms of understanding the implications of communion, there has been an interesting discussion around the topic of 'Responsible Communion' and what this can be said to mean. 'Responsible Communion' addresses issues such as the way in which it is possible to translate God's gift of communion into taking on responsibility together for the many issues that face us in today's world. Communion is not seen as 'otherworldly' or as 'churchly' in the sense of making a separation between church and world, but as enabling the Gospel of Christ to be taken forward in the world.

Conclusion

This paper points to the significance of the Holy Spirit shaping a communion among us which reflects the relational identity of the Holy Trinity. Openness to the Holy Spirit is a key attribute of Receptive Ecumenism, leading separated churches to recognise the gifts of the Holy Spirit in one another, and to be drawn closer to the one triune God. This possibility of a greater closeness to God is sought, both for the renewal of churches as they see what is common in their origins, and are drawn towards the same ultimate destination, and for a more effective witness to the Gospel, in word and action, in a needy world.

Bibliography

Barr, William R and Rena M Yocom, editors, *The Church in the Movement of the Spirit* (Grand Rapids, MI: Eerdmans, 1994).

Bergen, Jeremy M, 'The Holy Spirit and Lived Communion from the Perspective of International Bilateral Dialogues', in *Journal of Ecumenical Studies*, 49/2 (2014): 193–217.

Berger, Teresa and Bryan D Spinks, editors, *The Spirit in Worship, Worship in the Spirit* (Collegeville, MN: Liturgical Press, 2009).

Berkhof, Hendrikus, *The Doctrine of the Holy Spirit* (Richmond, VA: Westminster John Knox Press, 1986).

Buckley, James Joyce and David S Yeago, *Knowing the Triune God: the Work of the Spirit in the Practices of the Church* (Grand Rapids, MI: Eerdmans, 2001).

Congar, Yves, *I Believe in the Holy Spirit* (London: Geoffrey Chapman, 1983).

Fee, Gordon D, *The Holy Spirit in the Letters of Paul* (Peabody, MA: Hendrickson, 1994).

Fox, Patricia A, *God as Communion: John Zizioulas, Elizabeth Johnson, and the retrieval of the Symbol of the Triune God* (Collegeville, MN: Liturgical Press, 2001).

Gabriel, Andrew K, *The Lord is the Spirit: The Holy Spirit and the Divine Attributes* (Cambridge: James Clarke & Co, 2012).

Hendry, George S, *The Holy Spirit in Christian Theology* (London: SCM, 1964).

Heron, Alasdair, *The Holy Spirit* (London: Marshall, Morgan and Scott, 1983).

Jensen, Robert, *The Triune Identity* (Philadelphia PA: Fortress Press, 1982).

Kärkkäinen, Veli-Matti, *Pneumatology: the Holy Spirit in Ecumenical, International, and Contextual Perspective* (Grand Rapids, MI: Baker Academic, 2002).

Lacugna, Catherine Mowry, *God for us, the Trinity and Christian Life* (New York: HarperCollins 1991).

McIntyre, John, *The Shape of Pneumatology* (London: T&T Clark International, 2004).

Moule, CFD, *The Holy Spirit* (London: Mowbray, 1978).

Quash, Ben, *Found Theology: History, Imagination and the Holy Spirit* (London: Bloomsbury, 2013).

Rogers, EF, *After the Spirit: a Constructive Pneumatology from resources outside the modern West* (London: SCM, 2006).

Schmemann, Alexander, *For the Life of the World* (Crestwood NY: St Vladimir's Seminary Press 1973).

Thiselton, Anthony C, *The Holy Spirit: in Biblical Teaching, through the Centuries and Today* (Grand Rapids, MI: Eerdmans, 2013).

Towards a Symphony of Instruments, A Historical and Theological Consideration of the Instruments of Communion of the Anglican Communion, Inter-Anglican Standing Commission on Unity, Faith and Order, a working paper (2015).

Welker, Michael, *God the Spirit* (Eugene, OR: Wipf and Stock 2013).

Zizioulas, John, *Being as Communion* (London: Darton, Longman & Todd Ltd, 2004).

.

A Forum for Theology in the World Vol 5 No 2/2018

Receptive Ecumenical Learning:
A Constructive Way of Approaching Ecclesial
Identity and Renewal

Antonia Pizzey

The Catholic Church appears to be facing a period of renewal both in Australia and globally. The process of renewal necessarily entails a deep focus on interior concerns, an examination of the inner workings of the Church, and a consideration of problems and issues facing the Catholic community more broadly. It essentially involves issues and questions of identity: who are we, as the Catholic Church? In Australia, the upcoming Plenary Council in 2020 will focus on the Church in the twenty-first century. It is a timely response to Pope Francis' call for a listening church, especially in the wake of the Royal Commission into Institutional Responses to Child Sexual Abuse. The purpose of the Plenary Council is expressed as a 'Listening to God by listening to one another.'[1] It is an opportunity to discuss real challenges facing the Church, both internally and more broadly in Australian society and culture. It also highlights the need for dialogue and learning at three different levels: between Church and broader society; between Catholics and our ecumenical others; and most relevant here, for intra-Catholic dialogue and learning.

Lying beneath this push towards inner reflection and renewal are fundamental questions, such as, 'What does it mean to be Catholic today? How can the Church listen effectively to the Spirit's prompting and guidance? How can we receive new insights and learnings into the Catholic tradition?' Church renewal requires listening, active learning, and openness to the promptings of the Spirit, while maintaining integrity with the witness of Scripture and tradition; clearly,

---

1. Australian Catholic Bishops Conference, 'Plenary Council 2020 Welcome', *Plenary Council* <http://plenarycouncil.catholic.org.au/>, accessed 5 May 2018.

no simple or straightforward process. What methods can be used to help guide this process? Reflecting on ecumenical methods in general may be helpful when approaching processes of church renewal, such as the Plenary Council, especially considering the internal diversity of the Catholic Church. After all, as Geraldine Smyth points out, 'within the Roman Catholic Church, as with other churches and ecclesial communions, beliefs are neither univocally nor unanimously held.'[2] There is also a vital link between ecclesial reform and ecumenism, as Thomas Reese attests: 'In the past, we used to see reform of the Roman Catholic Church as essential to ecumenical progress. Today, the reverse is also true: ecumenism is an essential path to church reform.'[3] There is a need for Catholics from different spectrums of the faith to fruitfully dialogue with each other. How can Receptive Ecumenism, a ground-breaking ecumenical approach focusing on ecclesial learning and conversion, be helpful as a way to approach church life and renewal in the twenty-first century, even beyond specifically ecumenical concerns? This essay aims to reflect on how Receptive Ecumenism may offer a constructive way to approach Church renewal. To this end, firstly, Receptive Ecumenism's approach to ecclesial learning will be discussed, before moving on to examine a key obstacle to ecclesial learning, that of issues surrounding ecclesial identity. Finally, Receptive Ecumenism's positive approach to engaging with ecclesial identity will be explored.

Receptive Ecumenism is essentially a strategy of active ecclesial learning and listening in the service of institutional renewal. Instead of focusing externally on what other churches need to learn or where they need to change in order to bring the divided churches closer together and to Christ, Receptive Ecumenism focuses, instead, internally on what *our* church needs to learn, and how we need to be open

---

2. Geraldine Smyth, 'Jerusalem, Athens, and Zurich—Psychoanalytic Perspectives on Factors Inhibiting Receptive Ecumenism', in *Receptive Ecumenism and the Call to Catholic Learning: Exploring a Way for Contemporary Ecumenism*, edited by Paul D Murray (Oxford: Oxford University Press, 2008), 290.

3. Thomas J Reese, 'Organizational Factors Inhibiting Receptive Catholic Learning', in *Receptive Ecumenism and the Call to Catholic Learning: Exploring a Way for Contemporary Ecumenism*, edited by Paul D Murray (Oxford: Oxford University Press, 2008), 354.

to change in the Spirit to grow closer to Christ and to each other.[4] It places the responsibility for ecclesial learning and transformation back on to us, requiring us to engage in self-critical, humble, and yet also hope-filled learning. Receptive Ecumenism's focus on learning is key to Pope Francis' call for a 'listening church,' which engages in 'a mutual listening in which everyone has something to learn.'[5] This learning is ultimately directed at deepening, rather than diminishing, our own ecclesial identities. As Murray explains, engaging in Receptive Ecumenism is not 'a matter of becoming less Catholic but of becoming more Catholic precisely by becoming more appropriately Anglican, more appropriately Lutheran, more appropriately Methodist, more appropriately Orthodox . . . '.[6] It is a method which proposes that engaging in dialogue and listening will lead us to a deeper understanding of our own identity. Engaging in dialogue also carries the related task of appraising where our tradition may require reform, as Vatican II's Decree on Ecumenism states, 'all are led to examine their own faithfulness to Christ's will for the Church and, wherever necessary undertake with vigour the task of renewal and reform.'[7] What makes Receptive Ecumenism so distinctive compared to other dialogue approaches is that it focuses specifically on ecclesial learning and transformation, in the service of reform.

Receptive Ecumenism was officially launched in the form of an international colloquium held at Durham University in 2006 which focused on Receptive Ecumenism and Catholic learning, followed by further successful international conferences in 2009, 2014, and 2017.[8] The main driver behind Receptive Ecumenism is Professor

---

4. Paul D Murray, 'Receptive Ecumenism and Catholic Learning—Establishing the Agenda', in *Receptive Ecumenism and the Call to Catholic Learning: Exploring a Way for Contemporary Ecumenism*, edited by Paul D Murray (Oxford: Oxford University Press, 2008), 12.
5. Pope Francis, 'Address given Commemorating the 50th Anniversary of the Institution of the Synod of Bishops', 17 October 2015 <http://w2.vatican.va/content/francesco/en/speeches/2015/october/documents/papa-francesco_20151017_50-anniversario-sinodo.html>, accessed 5 May 2018.
6. Murray, 'Receptive Ecumenism and Catholic Learning', 16.
7. Vatican II Council, '*Unitatis Redintegratio*: Decree on Ecumenism', 4, in *Vatican Council II: The Basic Sixteen Documents: Constitutions, Decrees, Declarations*, edited by Austin Flannery (New York: Costello Publishing Company, 1996).
8. The first and second international conferences were held in 2006 and 2009 by the Department of Religion and Theology at Durham University in collaboration

Paul Murray. Murray was inspired by Paul Couturier, Walter Kasper and Rowan Williams' focus on spiritual ecumenism.[9] In developing Receptive Ecumenism, Murray seeks to reclaim the full ramifications of Couturier's vision of spiritual ecumenism, which properly extends to ecclesial and institutional conversion, not just personal or individual conversion.[10] This focus on ecclesial conversion, or ecclesial learning has significant implications as it seeks to involve the entire church community, in some way, in the process of Spirit-led renewal.[11] Receptive Ecumenism takes seriously Vatican II's call that ecumenism is a matter of 'interior conversion', leading a church tradition more deeply into itself.[12] Receptive Ecumenism emphasises the spirituality underlying ecumenism itself, seeking a balance between practical and theological ecumenism, which has points of relevance for discussing church renewal.

There have been two major, and at times opposing, streams in the ecumenical movement: theological ecumenism, focusing on doctrinal consensus (an ecumenism of the head), and practical ecumenism, focusing on cooperation (an ecumenism of the hands). These two streams, Faith and Order, and Life and Work, respectively, were

---

with Ushaw College, UK. The third conference was jointly held by the Center for Catholic Studies at Fairfield University CT, USA and the Centre for Catholic Studies at Durham University, UK in 2014. The fourth international conference was held in 2017 at Canberra, Australia, organised by the Centre for Ecumenical Studies as part of the Australian Centre for Christianity and Culture (Charles Sturt University), together with The Australian Catholic University's Institute for Religion and Critical Inquiry, and the Research Centre for Public and Contextual Theology.

9. See Paul D Murray and Andrea L Murray, 'The Roots, Range and Reach of Receptive Ecumenism', in *Unity in Process: Reflections on Ecumenism*, edited by Clive Barrett (London: Darton, Longman and Todd, 2012) for a discussion of the developmental influences on Receptive Ecumenism, including Couturier, Kasper, and Rowan Williams.

10. Murray and Murray, 'The Roots, Range and Reach of Receptive Ecumenism', 85; Paul D Murray, 'Growing into the Fullness of Christ: Receptive Ecumenism as an Instrument of Ecclesial Conversion' (presentation, The Catholic Theological Society of America: Sixty-Eighth Annual Convention: Conversion, Miami, Florida, June 6–9, 2013).

11. Paul D Murray, 'Families of Receptive Theological Learning: Scriptural Reasoning, Comparative Theology, and Receptive Ecumenism', in *Modern Theology* 29/4 (2013): 90.

12. Vatican II, '*Unitatis Redintegratio*', 7.

brought together in the World Council of Churches, but finding a balance between the two has proven difficult.[13] Practical ecumenism has tended to dominate, a supremacy recognised in the famous slogan: 'doctrine divides, service unites.' But an overemphasis on cooperation can endanger the ecumenical drive towards renewal, as 'in cooperation, churches remain the same and expect to be received as they are (and to receive) others as they are.'[14] So the problem with an overemphasis on practical ecumenism is that it may lead to a downgrading of the ecumenical aim, which is full visible unity.[15] By contrast, focusing on renewal rather than cooperation leads churches through the, at times, difficult and challenging process of facing change and scrutinising areas for reform. As Raith writes, 'cooperation pursues unity while maintaining the ecclesial *status quo*; renewal pursues unity through transforming the status quo.'[16] While practical and theological matters are of vital importance for ecclesial renewal at this moment, especially for the Plenary Council, Receptive Ecumenism reminds us that the overarching purpose of ecclesial renewal is deepened conversion into Christ. Receptive Ecumenism, while affirming the continued importance of both practical and theological ecumenism, directs our attention beyond learning about each other (theological ecumenism) *and* beyond simply cooperating with each other (practical ecumenism), to focus on learning *from* each other (receptive ecumenism). This is not to disregard the significance and value of theological and practical ecumenism, but rather to affirm that a balanced approach is necessary for today's context. However, the contemporary context also presents particular obstacles to ecclesial learning.

Resistance to ecclesial change is complex, involving many factors.[17] However, one of the most significant challenges facing eccle-

---

13. R David Nelson and Charles Raith, *Ecumenism: A Guide for the Perplexed* (Bloomsbury T&T Clark, 2017), 154.

14. Nelson and Raith, *Ecumenism*, 150.

15. Paul D Murray and Paula Gooder, 'Receptive Ecumenism and ARCIC III', Seminar in Celebration of the 50th Anniversary of the Visit of Archbishop Michael Ramsey to Pope Paul VI (Gregorian University, Rome, 2016).

16. Nelson and Raith, *Ecumenism*, 150.

17. Gerard Kelly, 'What is Receptive Ecumenism?', in *The Gift of Each Other: Learning from Other Christians*, edited by Gideon Goosen (Sydney: The New South Wales Ecumenical Council, 2013), 5–7.

sial learning and church renewal today is that of ecclesial identity.[18] Smyth points out that 'The recent resurgence of identity discourse has been spectacular.'[19] Globalisation, pluralism, secularism, and postmodern fluidity are some of the factors behind this trend, making identity at once both more important and also more fragmented and elusive. As Smyth expresses, 'The questions, "Who am I?" and "Where do I belong?" prompt further self-concern about "Which identity fits my changing, unstable situation?".'[20] Ecclesial identity is of vital concern for all churches. As Kasper explains, 'Even in a world which is characterized by globalization, many ask: Who are we? Who am I? Nobody wants to be absorbed in an anonymous and faceless whole.'[21] Considering the central importance of identity, it is unsurprising, as Avis makes clear, that 'as historic institutions, churches guard their identity.'[22] A church's identity is developed and strengthened by drawing on their historic contexts, their standpoints on key issues, such as gender and ministry, and their beliefs about relating to God. Ecclesial identity correspondingly shapes the approach churches take to the daily lives of their communities, to key issues, such as abortion or ministry, and vitally, creates a sense of belonging, binding the community together. Deborah Weissman writes that 'Particularism is what gives us roots, identity, a sense of belonging . . . Our particular identities have shaped our language, symbols, festivals, customs, foods, clothing, literature, music, and lifestyles.'[23] This sense of identity and belonging is crucially important in our pluralist and secular world. This is perhaps especially so for a church as global

---

18. James Sweeney, 'Receptive Ecumenism, Ecclesial Learning, and the "Tribe"', in *Receptive Ecumenism and the Call to Catholic Learning: Exploring a Way for Contemporary Ecumenism*, edited by Paul D Murray (Oxford: Oxford University Press, 2008), 334.

19. Geraldine Smyth, 'Jerusalem, Athens, and Zurich—Psychoanalytic Perspectives on Factors Inhibiting Receptive Ecumenism,' in *Receptive Ecumenism and the Call to Catholic Learning: Exploring a Way for Contemporary Ecumenism*, edited by Paul D Murray (Oxford: Oxford University Press, 2008), 294.

20. Smyth, 'Jerusalem, Athens, and Zurich', 294.

21. Walter Kasper, *That They May All Be One: The Call to Unity Today* (London: Burns & Oates, 2004), 15.

22. Paul Avis, *Reshaping Ecumenical Theology: The Church Made Whole?* (London: Continuum International Publishing Group, 2010), 19.

23. Deborah Weissman, 'Tribalism with a Human Face', in *Journal of Ecumenical Studies* 52/1 (2017): 175.

and internally diverse as the Catholic Church. Identity is therefore a key unifying factor. Anything that threatens that perceived unity and identity, such as ecumenical or even renewal processes, may be resisted or repudiated.

The problem is that ecclesial identity can become too dependent on one or two critical issues, making it both rigid and resistant to change, and actually diminishing the fullness of a tradition's identity. The response from some American Catholics to Pope Francis' 2018 apostolic exhortation, *Gaudete et Exsultatea*, highlights this issue. Francis writes that:

> . . . the life of the Church can become a museum piece or the possession of a select few. This can occur when some groups of Christians give excessive importance to certain rules, customs or ways of acting. The Gospel then tends to be reduced and constricted, deprived of its simplicity, allure and savour . . . It can affect groups, movements and communities, and it explains why so often they begin with an intense life in the Spirit, only to end up fossilized . . . or corrupt.[24]

He goes on to affirm the importance of defending 'the innocent unborn,' followed by stating that 'equally sacred, however, are the lives of the poor, those already born, the destitute, the abandoned and the underprivileged, the vulnerable infirm and elderly exposed to covert euthanasia, the victims of human trafficking, new forms of slavery, and every form of rejection.'[25] He emphasises that holiness requires attention to all issues of injustice.[26] However, for some American Catholics, abortion is the preeminent issue, an essential part of their identity as Catholics, which explains some of the backlash to the document.[27] Such a reaction is expressed by anti-abortion

---

24. Pope Francis, *Gaudete et Exsultatea*, apostolic exhortation given 19 March 2018, 58, *Vatican website*, <http://w2.vatican.va/content/francesco/en/apost_exhortations/documents/papa-francesco_esortazione-ap_20180319_gaudete-et-exsultate.html>, accessed 6 May 2018.

25. Francis, *Gaudete et Exsultatea*, 101.

26. Francis, *Gaudete et Exsultatea*, 101.

27. Christina Cauterucci, 'Pro-Lifers Dismiss Pope's Declaration that Protecting Migrants Is Just as Important as Abortion,' *Slate*, April 11 2018, <https://slate.com/news-and-politics/2018/04/pro-lifers-dont-seem-to-care-that-the-pope-said-immigrant-justice-is-just-as-important-as-abortion.html>, accessed May 6 2018:

activist Marjorie Dannenfesler, who states: 'It is impossible to equate the moral weight of abortion—the direct killing of innocent unborn children occurring on a daily massive scale, here in America and abroad—with any other social justice issue . . . The right to live pre-dates or precludes every other right . . . Today's exhortation blurs lines and causes confusion.'[28] There is a perception that, in this exhortation, Francis is criticising 'one issue' Catholicism, referring to the narrowing of Catholic identity down to any one issue, such as abortion.[29] Pope Francis' 2016 apostolic exhortation *Amoris Laetitia* experienced a similar backlash on the issue of giving communion to divorced and remarried Catholics, causing serious controversy in the Church. If identity rests too dependently on one issue it risks becoming brittle, and ultimately, weak, unable to adapt to different contexts. A static, or 'hardened identity',[30] is therefore a challenge for ecclesial learning.

For both ecumenism and renewal, ecclesial identity can be a barrier to learning if there is a perception that the aim is to diminish identity. Differences serve to distinguish a church's identity from others, such as how the Petrine ministry contributes to Catholic identity.[31] The process of renewal, where ways of thinking and practising are scrutinised, therefore can be seen as potentially threatening the community's identity. Raith explains that many 'refused to participate in ecumenical work because they equate such work with syncretism, the clumsy attempt to create unity at the expense of truth'. They therefore refuse dialogue on the belief that it 'might compromise the integrity of their own positions'. However, as he explains, 'True ecumenical learning blooms when dialoguing churches allow each other to challenge each other's assumptions about the nature and content of Christian truth'.[32] A rigid understanding of identity is not conducive to learning. James Sweeney offers a sociological take on Catholicism, explaining that over the last forty years, the Catholic Church 'has begun to

---

28. Quoted in Cauterucci, 'Pro-Lifers Dismiss Pope's Declaration that Protecting Migrants Is Just as Important as Abortion'.
29. Tara Isabella Burton, 'Pope Francis: Catholics should care as much about the poor as about abortion,' *Vox*, April 11 2018, <https://www.vox.com/2018/4/11/17220108/pope-francis-catholics-conservative-abortion-gaudete-exsultate-twitter-church-apostolic-exhortation>, accessed 6 May 2018.
30. Smyth, 'Jerusalem, Athens, and Zurich', 294.
31. Avis, *Reshaping Ecumenical Theology*, 19.
32. Nelson and Raith, *Ecumenism*, 144–5.

transcend its self-imposed institutional impregnability', known as 'the fortress church—a Catholicism closed to external sources of learning and content in its ideological self-sufficiency'.[33] However, the 'fortress' mentality is still a factor, as rigidity over ecclesial identity, expressed by an excessive assertion of identity which leaves no room for learning or change, seems to be a growing trend.[34] It is sometimes referred to as reconfessionalism. Murray calls it a 'post-modern heightening of the particularity of identity over against any easily assumed commonality'.[35] Reconfessionalism is not necessarily an unreasonable reaction, especially when churches are faced with hostile milieus, and therefore seek to protect and safeguard themselves by drawing away from engagement and dialogue. However, Gerard Kelly clarifies that 'renewed confessionalism' is negative 'if it builds walls around churches, effectively entrenching division'.[36] While Kelly is referring specifically to ecumenical dialogue, something similar can be said for church renewal, especially regarding renewal for a church as diverse as the Catholic Church. Listening requires a lowering of walls and an openness to consider different points of view—and to reconsider our own.

Effective dialogue and engagement is critical for any process of renewal, not just for the Catholic Church but for Christianity as a whole. Sweeney argues that 'churches will only re-establish their role in late modern society if they succeed in cultivating a reflexive and self-critical identity, humble enough and secure enough to engage in dialogue'.[37] As such, negative reconfessionalism is of concern not only to ecumenism, but for the whole church. However, on the more positive side, renewal processes, arduous as they may be, actually aim towards the renewal of ecclesial identities. The renewed ecclesial identity is hoped to represent 'a more authentic expression of church

---

33. James Sweeney, 'Receptive Ecumenism, Ecclesial Learning, and the 'Tribe', in *Receptive Ecumenism and the Call to Catholic Learning: Exploring a Way for Contemporary Ecumenism*, edited by Paul D Murray (Oxford: Oxford University Press, 2008), 334.

34. Annemarie Mayer, 'The Ecumenical Vision of Pope Francis: Journeying Together as Fellow Pilgrims—"the Mystery of Unity Has Already Begun"', in *International Journal for the Study of the Christian Church*, 17/3, (2017): 161.

35. Paul D Murray, 'Receptive Ecumenism and Ecclesial Learning: Receiving Gifts for Our Needs', in *Louvain Studies*, 33/1–2, (2008): 35.

36. Kelly, 'Receptive Ecumenism', 4.

37. Sweeney, 'Receptive Ecumenism, Ecclesial Learning, and the "Tribe"', 343.

life, learning from the richness of the whole *oikumene*.[38] Any process that appears to denigrate or diminish identity is therefore suspect, but the pitfalls of rigid defensiveness must also be avoided. What might we able to learn from Receptive Ecumenism to aid us in engaging issues surrounding ecclesial identity?

Receptive Ecumenism is acutely aware of the need to protect ecclesial identity. As Örsy makes clear, ecclesial learning can only be authentic if it supports a church's identity.[39] Grounded in this concern, Receptive Ecumenism seeks not to detract, but rather to enrich, ecclesial identity through engagement with others. In an article based on her paper at the 2009 Receptive Ecumenism conference, Catherine Clifford offers valuable insight into how Receptive Ecumenism approaches the challenge of ecclesial identity.[40] She identifies the tensions surrounding ecclesial identity and change as being grounded in a sense of insecurity, as churches ask: 'Can we possibly change without sacrificing something that is essential, that defines us as who we are as Orthodox, Catholic, Anglican, or Protestant Christians, without betraying a tradition that has been entrusted to us by the apostles?'[41] In tackling this insecurity, she emphasises the work of the *Groupe des Dombes*[42] in asserting that 'some of what needs correcting is our very sense of self, our sense of identity, which has too often confounded confessional identity or self with the identity or self of the one church of Christ.'[43] There are eschatological overtones here, in the need to

---

38. Kelly, 'Receptive Ecumenism', 4.
39. Ladislas Örsy, 'Authentic *Learning* and *Receiving*—A Search for Criteria', in *Receptive Ecumenism and the Call to Catholic Learning: Exploring a Way for Contemporary Ecumenism*, edited by Paul D Murray (Oxford: Oxford University Press, 2008), 42.
40. Catherine E Clifford, 'Kenosis and the Church: Putting on the Mind of Christ', in *One in Christ*, 43/2 (2009): 2–5.
41. Clifford, 'Kenosis and the Church', 2.
42. Couturier also established the influential ecumenical group the *Groupe des Dombes* in 1937. The *Groupe* is remarkable for being 'the longest standing forum for Protestant-Catholic ecumenical dialogue', according to Clifford, *The Groupe Des Dombes*, 1. The *Groupe des Dombes* emphasises spiritual ecumenism, focusing on ecclesial conversion. For an English translation of some of their most important documents, see Catherine Clifford, editor, *For the Communion of the Churches: The Contribution of the Groupe Des Dombes* (Grand Rapids, MI: Eerdmans, 2010).
43. Clifford, 'Kenosis and the Church', 4.

recognise that there is a difference between the Church of Christ and our earthly churches. As she explains:

> The impulse to retrenchment in denominational identities reveals that we have at times reversed the order of priority and placed the sense of confessional identity above fidelity to the church of Christ, or confused historically and culturally conditioned forms of doctrine and church practice with the timeless tradition of the apostolic faith.[44]

Acknowledging the eschatological incompleteness of the church provides a way of being receptive, rather than defensive, regarding ecclesial identity. What is truly essential to our identity is our relationship to Christ, our fidelity to him as his body on earth—rather than any one issue, no matter how important, such as abortion or divorced and remarried Catholics. On this point, she explains that, 'To move forward on the path of receptive ecumenism we must have the humility to make an honest assessment of where our churches may have a distorted perception of their ecclesial selves'.[45] This is the real challenge and potential reward of Receptive Ecumenical learning, as Murray explains that 'ecumenical theological learning should be about the enrichment rather than diminishment of identity. This is a great gift to bestow: to help another become him/herself in all his/her difference from you.'[46] Receptive Ecumenism aims towards a deepening of conversion, and thus of ecclesial identity. He emphasises that, 'It is a process of growth and change—a process of conversion—that is at root not a loss, nor a diminishment but a finding, a freeing, an intensification, and an enrichment.'[47] Emphasising this point even further, Clifford argues that churches 'might need to be freed from a false sense of self,' and that 'these false selves' must 'be emptied,' and replaced with the mind of Christ.[48] 'Every faith community must pass through this kenotic way if we are to grow in genuine communion,' she says.[49] Ecumenism, as she puts it, calls for 'the churches to move from being self-centered, or confessionally-centered, to adopt-

---

44. Clifford, 'Kenosis and the Church', 5.
45. Clifford, 'Kenosis and the Church', 5.
46. Murray and Murray, 'The Roots, Range and Reach of Receptive Ecumenism', 82.
47. Murray, 'Receptive Ecumenism and Catholic Learning', 6.
48. Clifford, 'Kenosis and the Church', 5.
49. Clifford, 'Kenosis and the Church', 5.

ing a sense of church that is Christ-centered.'[50] Ecclesial identity must therefore be viewed through the lens of Christ. It is to Christ's identity that we must conform, and it is Christ's identity which cannot be compromised or sacrificed. We must allow Christ and the Spirit to 'become the criteria for our unity in the place of our particular ecclesial selves.'[51]

Murray's and Clifford's views echo those of Yves Congar, who attests that, far from any risk of losing our ecclesial identities through undertaking ecumenism, ecumenical engagement and interior conversion leads us to a deepened and more truthful realisation of ourselves in Christ. Congar believes that engaging in dialogue allows us to rediscover 'parts of our heritage of which we never dreamed,' to recover parts 'of our common heritage which our separated brethren retained in parting from us and which they have perceived, developed and lived with greater intensity than we have.' Ultimately, it will mean a 'rediscovery, in greater depth and breadth, of our own tradition.'[52] Congar recognises how difficult such a self-critical process can be.

> Yet, painful as such an effort is, it soon reaps its reward in the expansion of our own catholicity and in countless discoveries and enrichments. Beyond the purely confessional and somewhat narrow meaning of that fine name 'catholic', we shall discover a truer sense of what we are and learn to become all that name implies, to make it a reality rather than a mere label and ourselves become more 'catholic', more 'universal.'[53]

In line with the work of the *Groupe des Dombes*, Murray attests that it requires 'traditions to relinquish the rigid absolutizing of their opposed confessional identities,' and recognise what gifts can be received from other traditions.[54] However, any learning or change

50. Clifford, 'Kenosis and the Church', 5.
51. Clifford, 'Kenosis and the Church', 5.
52. Yves Congar, *Dialogue Between Christians: Catholic Contributions to Ecumenism*, translated by Philip Loretz (London: Geoffrey Chapman, 1966), 105.
53. Congar, *Dialogue Between Christians*, 105.
54. Paul D Murray, 'Growing into the Fullness of Christ: Receptive Ecumenism as an Instrument of Ecclesial Conversion.' Presented at *The Catholic Theological Society of America: Sixty-Eighth Annual Convention: Conversion*, Miami, Florida, 6–9 June 2013.

which takes place through ecclesial learning must be authentic, which involves a process of discernment.

In order for a tradition to be open to change, there needs to be a self-critical and imaginative consideration of where renewal needs to occur.[55] This discernment involves the whole church, as Murray makes clear that every member of the church can be involved in different ways at different levels.[56] However, the engagement of theologians, experts and ecclesial leaders is also necessarily required to ensure 'rigorous and sophisticated theological scrutiny, testing and discernment' so that authentic and coherent growth can be fostered.[57] But even above all of this, conversion is not possible via human effort alone; it requires us to be open to, and even 'lean into' the Spirit's will, as Murray asserts.[58]

The virtues of love and humility play a necessary part in developing the predisposition to prepare a church to engage in ecclesial learning. Geraldine Hawkes affirms that 'Receptive Ecumenism requires a disposition of love and humility.'[59]

Both virtues receive explicit emphasis in Receptive Ecumenism. Murray attests that love is 'the way of ecclesial transformation'.[60] This statement resonates with *Unitatis Redintegratio*'s conviction that love must receive priority above all else.[61] Love orientates us towards Christ, as the impetus behind renewal is, as his community, to, draw closer to him. Love is essential to change and renewal, as Murray expresses, 'we are changed by love not by anger and if we are in turn to effect creative ecclesial change then it must be through the sustained passion of love rather than frustration.'[62]

55. Kelly, 'What is Receptive Ecumenism?', 7.
56. Murray, 'Families of Receptive Theological Learning', 90.
57. Murray, 'Families of Receptive Theological Learning', 90.
58. Paul D Murray, 'Vatican II: On Celebrating Vatican II as Catholic and Ecumenical', in *The Second Vatican Council: Celebrating its Achievements and the Future*, edited by Gavin D'Costa and Emma Jane Harris (London: Bloomsbury T&T Clark, 2013), 85–104, 99.
59. Geraldine Hawkes, 'Receptive Ecumenism: Encounter with Beauty, Truth and Love', presentation, South Australian Council of Churches Annual Ecumenical Lecture, (Adelaide College of Divinity, Adelaide, 2013).
60. Murray and Murray, 'The Roots, Range and Reach of Receptive Ecumenism', 89.
61. Vatican II, 'Unitatis Redintegratio', 4.
62. Murray and Murray, 'The Roots, Range and Reach of Receptive Ecumenism', 89.

Humility is also vital to Receptive Ecumenical learning. It requires us to have the humility to recognise areas where we need to repent for our failings. It is needed to guide us in self-critical discernment of areas in need of reform, and to lead us towards authentic willingness to listen to others. As Avis asserts, 'The witness of RE is needed to remind all churches that they are wounded and incomplete and need to be made whole by divine mercy'.[63] Humility is not, however, about thinking less of our own tradition or adopting a false modesty, but is rather about having a true understanding of ourselves.[64] Humility is necessary to avoid ecclesial arrogance, as seen in the 'fortress church' mentality, where we refuse to listen and consider the resources proffered by those from another viewpoint. As Smyth states, learning involves the 'need for the church to go beyond egoism in order to learn from different perspectives, to compromise sufficiently to listen and eschew self-sufficiency'.[65] The last point, on self-sufficiency, is particularly relevant to Receptive Ecumenism, as it advocates a humble approach of showing each other our weaknesses, our 'wounded hands,' thereby cultivating ecclesial humility, instead of the more usual approach of presenting our best selves, which could lead to ecclesial arrogance.[66] This ecclesial humility is vital to renewal. As Raith explains:

> When ecumenical work is animated by a spirit of humility, service, and love, genuine ecumenical learning, in service to the truth of the apostolic faith, becomes possible. However, the process of ecumenical reception forestalls when the absence of love in the face of the other is married to pride in the truth claims of one's own tradition.[67]

Ecclesial arrogance militates against an attitude of learning and receptiveness, which can lead to a refusal to genuinely engage in renewal processes altogether.

---

63. Paul Avis, 'Are We Receiving 'Receptive Ecumenism'?', in *Ecclesiology* 8/2 (2012): 232.
64. Josef Pieper, *Fortitude and Temperance*, translated by Daniel F Coogan (London: Faber and Faber, 1955), 106.
65. Smyth, 'Jerusalem, Athens and Zurich', 291.
66. Murray, 'Growing into the Fullness of Christ'.
67. Nelson and Raith, *Ecumenism*, 144.

In conclusion, ecclesial identity is the bedrock of our Church communities, acting as an important unifying factor and cultivating a sense of belonging, which is crucially important today. Yet, we must also safeguard our identities so that they do not become rigid and incapable of learning. Receptive Ecumenism offers a helpful strategy worthy of reflection when grappling with issues surrounding ecclesial identity and learning, applicable to both specifically ecumenical questions of renewal and renewal more broadly.

Bibliography

Australian Catholic Bishops Conference, 'Plenary Council 2020 Welcome', Plenary Council at <http://plenarycouncil.catholic.org.au/>, accessed 5 May 2018.

Avis, Paul, 'Are We Receiving "Receptive Ecumenism?"' in *Ecclesiology*, 8/2 (2012): 223–34.

——*Reshaping Ecumenical Theology: The Church Made Whole*? (London: Continuum International Publishing Group, 2010).

Burton, Tara Isabella, 'Pope Francis: Catholics should care as much about the poor as about abortion', *Vox*, April 11 2018 <https://www.vox.com/2018/4/11/17220108/pope-francis-catholics-conservative-abortion-gaudete-exsultate-twitter-church-apostolic-exhortation>, accessed 6 May 2018.

Cauterucci, Christina, 'Pro-Lifers Dismiss Pope's Declaration that Protecting Migrants Is Just as Important as Abortion', *Slate*, April 11 2018 <https://slate.com/news-and-politics/2018/04/pro-lifers-dont-seem-to-care-that-the-pope-said-immigrant-justice-is-just-as-important-as-abortion.html>, accessed 6 May 2018.

Clifford, Catherine E, 'Kenosis and the Church: Putting on the Mind of Christ', in *One in Christ*, 43/2 (2009): 2–5.

——editor, *For the Communion of the Churches: The Contribution of the Groupe Des Dombes* (Grand Rapids, MI: Eerdmans, 2010).

Congar, Yves, *Dialogue Between Christians: Catholic Contributions to Ecumenism*, translated by Philip Loretz (London: Geoffrey Chapman, 1966).

Hawkes, Geraldine, 'Receptive Ecumenism: Encounter with Beauty, Truth and Love', South Australian Council of Churches Annual Ecumenical Lecture (Adelaide College of Divinity, Adelaide, 2013).

Kasper, Walter, *That They May All Be One: The Call to Unity Today* (London: Burns & Oates, 2004).

Kelly, Gerard, 'What is Receptive Ecumenism?', in *The Gift of Each Other: Learning from Other Christians*, edited by Gideon Goosen (Sydney: The New South Wales Ecumenical Council, 2013), 5–7.

Mayer, Annemarie, 'The Ecumenical Vision of Pope Francis: Journeying Together as Fellow Pilgrims—"the Mystery of Unity Has Already Begun"', in *International Journal for the Study of the Christian Church*, 17/3 (2017): 156–72.

Murray, Paul D, 'Families of Receptive Theological Learning: Scriptural Reasoning, Comparative Theology, and Receptive Ecumenism', in *Modern Theology*, 29/4 (2013): 76–92.

——'Growing into the Fullness of Christ: Receptive Ecumenism as an Instrument of Ecclesial Conversion' (presentation, The Catholic Theological Society of America: Sixty-Eighth Annual Convention: Conversion, Miami, Florida, June 6-9, 2013).

——'Receptive Ecumenism and Catholic Learning—Establishing the Agenda', in *Receptive Ecumenism and the Call to Catholic Learning: Exploring a Way for Contemporary Ecumenism*, edited by Paul D Murray (Oxford: Oxford University Press, 2008), 5–26.

——'Receptive Ecumenism and Ecclesial Learning: Receiving Gifts for Our Needs', in *Louvain Studies*, 33/1–2 (2008): 30–45.

——'Vatican II: On Celebrating Vatican II as Catholic and Ecumenical', in *The Second Vatican Council: Celebrating its Achievements and the Future*, edited by Gavin D'Costa and Emma Jane Harris (London: Bloomsbury T&T Clark, 2013), 85–104.

——and Paula Gooder, 'Receptive Ecumenism and ARCIC III', Seminar in Celebration of the 50th Anniversary of the Visit of Archbishop Michael Ramsey to Pope Paul VI (Gregorian University, Rome, 2016).

——and Andrea L Murray, 'The Roots, Range and Reach of Receptive Ecumenism', in *Unity in Process: Reflections on Ecumenism*, edited by Clive Barrett (London: Darton, Longman and Todd, 2012), 79–94.

Nelson, R David and Charles Raith, *Ecumenism: A Guide for the Perplexed* (Bloomsbury T&T Clark, 2017).

Örsy, Ladislas, 'Authentic Learning and Receiving—A Search for Criteria', in *Receptive Ecumenism and the Call to Catholic Learning:*

Exploring a Way for Contemporary Ecumenism, edited by Paul D Murray (Oxford: Oxford University Press, 2008), 39–51.

Pieper, Josef, *Fortitude and Temperance*, translated by Daniel F Coogan (London: Faber and Faber, 1955).

Pope Francis, 'Address given Commemorating the 50th Anniversary of the Institution of the Synod of Bishops', 17 October 2015: <http://w2.vatican.va/content/francesco/en/speeches/2015/october/documents/papa-francesco_20151017_50-anniversario-sinodo.html>, accessed 5 May 2018.

——*Gaudete et Exsultatea* 58, apostolic exhortation given 19 March 2018: <http://w2.vatican.va/content/francesco/en/apost_exhortations/documents/papa-francesco_esortazione-ap_20180319_gaudete-et-exsultate.html>, accessed 6 May 2018.

Reese, Thomas J, 'Organizational Factors Inhibiting Receptive Catholic Learning', in *Receptive Ecumenism and the Call to Catholic Learning: Exploring a Way for Contemporary Ecumenism*, edited by Paul D Murray (Oxford: Oxford University Press, 2008), 346–56.

Smyth, Geraldine, 'Jerusalem, Athens, and Zurich—Psychoanalytic Perspectives on Factors Inhibiting Receptive Ecumenism', in *Receptive Ecumenism and the Call to Catholic Learning: Exploring a Way for Contemporary Ecumenism*, edited by Paul D Murray (Oxford: Oxford University Press, 2008), 285–302.

Sweeney, James, 'Receptive Ecumenism, Ecclesial Learning, and the "Tribe"', in *Receptive Ecumenism and the Call to Catholic Learning: Exploring a Way for Contemporary Ecumenism*, edited by Paul D Murray (Oxford: Oxford University Press, 2008), 333–45.

Vatican II Council, '*Unitatis Redintegratio*: Decree on Ecumenism', in *Vatican Council II: The Basic Sixteen Documents: Constitutions, Decrees, Declarations*, edited by Austin Flannery (New York: Costello Publishing Company, 1996).

Weissman, Deborah, 'Tribalism with A Human Face', in *Journal of Ecumenical Studies*, 52/1 (2017): 169–77.

Applied Synodality and Contemporary Orthodox Diaspora: Learning from a Lutheran-Roman Catholic Document[1]

Doru Costache

In August 2007, the bilateral commission for Lutheran–Roman Catholic dialogue in Australia published *The Ministry of Oversight: The Office of Bishop and President in the Church*, the outcome of seven years of collaboration. The document is structured in seven chapters preceded by an introduction, which outlines the early Christian and medieval understanding of episcopal or oversight ministry, alongside its representations from the Reformation onwards, down to contemporary doctrines and practices. Further sections refer to the institution of oversight, its status as a gift to the Church, apostolic succession, the rapports between bishop and synod, and the pastoral dimension of episcopacy. Together with summarising the traditional views of both Roman Catholics and Lutherans, each chapter concludes with statements on the findings and recommendations submitted to the Churches represented. The resulting image of episcopal ministry is nuanced and shaped by ecclesial consideration. The document ends by mapping the current challenges and suggesting future steps to be taken in the dialogue.

Elsewhere, in a 2012 essay,[2] I addressed aspects pertaining to this document with which educated Eastern Orthodox readers may feel uneasy. Surmising their understanding from the concept of divine

---

1. I am grateful to The Revd Peter Balabanski for his stylistic suggestions, which improved the legibility of this essay. Text available at <http://www.cam.org.au/Portals/66/Resources/Documents/LutheranChurch/Ministry_of_Oversight2007.pdf>. Accessed 6 May 2018.
2. Doru Costache, 'Notes on *The Ministry of Oversight* Document.' Text available at <https://www.academia.edu/1467374/Notes_on_The_Ministry_of_Oversight_Document>. Accessed 6 May 2018.

humanity, central to the Eastern Orthodox framework, such readers would experience uneasiness regarding the disjunction of divine and human aspects in the document's articulation of episcopal institution. Indeed, this kind of disjunction is virtually inconceivable for a Church which considers the permanent co-operation of divine and human factors its cornerstone. The same goes for the juridical appraisal of episcopacy within the document, which is incompatible with the ecclesial mindset of Orthodox tradition. Together with the following, my 2012 observations may be of importance as a view from a third party, for whomever is interested in the reception of this document.

Herein I return to *The Ministry of Oversight* from the angle of receptive ecumenism, attempting to draw lessons for contemporary Orthodox experience in diaspora. So perceived, the document surprises Eastern Orthodox readers on several levels—from the humble approach of its authors to their realistic assessment of their own traditions and their capacity to recognise in the experience of their counterparts valid and shared aspects, beyond structural polymorphisms, failures, and historical differences. Such an approach is the very opposite of contemporary Orthodox triumphalism. Indeed, even a superficial browsing of official documents and ecclesiological monographs recently produced reveals that, with few exceptions, the Orthodox discourse is always about external challenges and never about internal difficulties. The established narrative is that everything is invariably well within the Orthodox Church, regardless of how blatantly obvious the problems may be. Since all is well, receptive ecumenism seems to be out of the question. Against this backdrop, Eastern Orthodox readers may be astonished by the approach of *The Ministry of Oversight* to episcopal ministry. Specifically, the document interprets episcopacy in ecclesial fashion, from the angle of synodality. In what follows I take synodality in the broadest of senses, namely, as corresponding to the catholicity affirmed by the Nicene-Constantinopolitan creed. In short, all that pertains to the Church presupposes the Church in its entirety. It seems to me that, beyond their differences, the two parties represented by *The Ministry of Oversight* are of this view. But this synodal or ecclesial assessment of episcopacy is at odds with the current situation in the Eastern Orthodox diaspora, which demonstrably lacks such a perspective. Specifically, on a diocesan level only seldom are there obvious synodical structures that secure the ecclesial grounding of episcopal authority. This impacts the pastoral and missionary activity dramatically. Also, the Eastern Orthodox Churches coexisting in diaspora do not cultivate fellowship. Furthermore, on an international scale, the recent Holy and Great Council of the Orthodox Church (Crete, 19–26 June 2016)[3] has revealed the disunity of the Eastern Orthodox family, the incapacity of its episcopacy to synodise or walk together (from the Greek συνοδεύω, whence σύνοδος, synod) in harmony. In various manners, I propose, these issues stem from two main causes, namely, the lack of synodality and the priority of ethnicity over what the Eastern Orthodox hold in common. Given these difficulties, triumphalism should be abandoned. Learning from *The Ministry of Oversight* may inspire ways to overcome such difficulties.

In what follows, taking as a case-study the situation in Australia, I reflect on the relevance of *The Ministry of Oversight* beyond the parties involved in its redaction. I propose that the document suggests solutions for the pastoral and missionary challenges that face contemporary Orthodox diaspora, challenges which cannot be overcome without retrieving the ecclesial mindset and the practice of synodality. Before anything though, an overview of the relevant material within the document is in order.

Lessons from *The Ministry of Oversight*

The writers involved in the redaction of *The Ministry of Oversight* seem to have been guided by such concerns as what they say about themselves and what they can learn from one another: questions typical for receptive ecumenism. Their approach is perfectly exemplified by several articles which treat the rapport between episcopal ministry and synodality, acknowledging what the two parties hold in common beyond the historical differences which have kept them apart. Here is an example of this approach:

---

3. For the official documents of and the debates around the Holy and Great Council of the Orthodox Church, see <https://www.holycouncil.org/>. Accessed 6 May 2018.

> While we both hold to the fundamental importance of
> synodal structures, we recognise that the history of our two
> communities has meant that there are differences between us
> on the practice of synodality. The Roman Catholic community
> has a strong conviction about the role of the bishop in the
> church. We suggest that the Lutheran community may have
> something to learn from this understanding of the bishop as
> the focus of unity of the church. The Lutheran community in
> Australia, and elsewhere, has a strong history of participation
> through synodical structures. We suggest that the Roman
> Catholic Church, as it attempts to bring about more effective
> participation, may have something to learn from the synodical
> practices of the Lutheran community.[4]

The passage points out that the two Churches have historically displayed different ecclesiological figures, one hierarchical—the Catholic Church—and one synodal—the Lutheran Church. But, as a
conclusion to Chapter 5: 'Bishops, Presidents and Synodality', which
focuses on the rapport between hierarchy and synodality in both
Churches, the above statement not only defines what pertains to each
ecclesial tradition, it also suggests what each can learn from the other.
Specifically, Lutherans should learn from the Catholics to appreciate
episcopal ministry as a factor of ecclesial unity, whereas Catholics
should learn from the Lutherans the importance of synodical practices for a fuller ecclesial participation. In recommending what each
tradition should learn from the other, the passage suggests that an
ideal Christian Church combines both principles, hierarchical and
synodal, and so preeminence and fellowship, authority and consultation. This ecclesiological model is the hallmark of a Church able to
avoid the pitfalls of despotism and fragmentation, neither of which is
of service to the Gospel.

The end of the document reaffirms the same conclusions by way
of concrete recommendations from the commission's members for
their respective Churches. Thus, 'the Roman Catholic members of
the dialogue ask their church authorities to consider that the Spirit
of God might be leading them to recognise the authenticity of the
Lutheran ministry'.[5] In turn, 'the Lutheran members . . . encourage

---

4. *The Ministry of Oversight*, 115.
5. *The Ministry of Oversight*, 133.

the Lutheran Church of Australia to recognise and uphold the distinctiveness and unifying role of the office of president/bishop, and to build upon, renew and deepen its understanding of the apostolic and catholic nature of the office.[6] These statements address the rapport discussed in Chapter 5 between episcopate and synodality only implicitly, by agreeing on the validity of the two models: namely, the Lutheran synodal structures and the Catholic hierarchical structures. Even so, they submit that when considered under the Spirit's guidance the two models complement each other. This conclusion is perfectly consistent with the findings outlined in Chapter 5, particularly article 115 quoted above.

I shall return to this exercise of mutual recognition in my attempt to draw wisdom for Eastern Orthodox diaspora. But what matters is that the above conclusions find confirmation in a statement which further discloses the spirit in which the members involved in the dialogue have worked. Here is the excerpt of interest.

> In different ways in the theology of both our churches there is an understanding that the apostolic ministry can be preserved in certain circumstances even when there are variations in structure.[7]

Addressing the main topic of the document, the article of which this statement is a part highlights the agreement of the dialogue's members on the apostolic nature of the two forms of leadership cultivated by their Churches. Thus, apostolicity is recognisable in both models notwithstanding their different organisational, hierarchical and synodal traditions. In stating this agreement, the passage confirms what has been discussed earlier. Equally important is that this statement conveys something fundamental about what led both parties to express mutual recognition: namely, the theological charism of prioritising what truly matters, against matters of secondary importance. Indeed, this statement and the other articles surveyed herein show the aptitude of the authors to perceive the truth beyond its circumstantial polymorphisms and their adherence to the principles of receptive ecumenism. This adherence presupposes the humble awareness of one's own limitations and the need to learn from the other's strengths.

---

6. *The Ministry of Oversight*, 134.
7. *The Ministry of Oversight*, 132.

To discuss the outcomes of the document is beyond the scope of this essay, but there is evidence that its guidelines are taken seriously by the concerned parties.[8] In what follows I point out what the Eastern Orthodox could learn from this document and from the mechanics of the dialogue that led to its creation. But before doing so, I offer a case-study: the condition of Orthodoxy in contemporary Australia.

Australian Orthodoxy

I take Australian Orthodoxy as a case-study given my familiarity with its circumstances. As far as I know, from research, first-hand experience, and personal contacts, most aspects discussed below are shared by the Eastern Orthodox diaspora throughout the world, with certain exceptions. I focus on the ecclesiastical units belonging to the Eastern Orthodox Churches present Down Under,[9] which perfectly illustrate the difficulties outlined in the introduction. Like everywhere else, these ecclesiastical units, untraditionally designated as jurisdictions, owe their origins to migration. But currently some are at the stage of timid indigenisation due to a shift in numbers in favour of their Australian-born members and converts. Each jurisdiction is organised according to the customs of its Church of origin and operates according to guidelines issued by their overseas headquarters. These guidelines are rooted in the nationalist ideologies of the nineteenth century, prioritising ethnic rather than Christian interests. Because of their commitment to such guidelines—a particularity replicated

---

8. I am grateful to Adam Cooper for providing the following information. After the release of the document, the Lutheran Church of Australia has changed the title of 'president' to 'bishop' for the district and national overseers. See <http://www.lca.org.au/departments/office-bishop/>. Accessed 22 March 2018. In turn, the Conference of the Australian Catholic Bishops prepares for a nation-wide plenary synod in 2020, to include the laity. See <http://catholicleader.com.au/news/brisbane-archbishop-calls-for-first-synod-for-entire-catholic-church-in-australia-since-1937>. Accessed 6 May 2018.

9. Michael Angold, editor, *The Cambridge History of Christianity*, volume 5: *Eastern Christianity* (Cambridge University Press, 2006). Ken Parry, editor, *The Blackwell Companion to Eastern Christianity* (Malden, Oxford, Carlton: Blackwell Publishing, 2007). These volumes are very important resources for the understanding of the origins and specificities of the Eastern Orthodox Churches represented in Australia, but they offer likewise details about Orthodox diaspora worldwide.

with little variation across the spectrum—the local jurisdictions do not favour indigenisation. More specifically, they do not engage their context in a missional sense, instead creating ethnic, cultural, and linguistic bubbles separated from one another, from other Christian Churches, and from Australian society at large. As the local jurisdictions insist on having their membership recorded by the census authorities, belonging with an Eastern Orthodox Church is not a matter of Orthodox Christianity; it is a matter of ethnic identity. No census rubric mentions Australian Orthodox or Eastern Orthodox, the way Roman Catholics and Lutherans register, without adding the ethnic background of the members. From a jurisdictional or institutional viewpoint therefore, literally and figuratively, the phrase Australian Orthodoxy is meaningless.

It is true that there is a recently established Assembly of Canonical Orthodox Bishops of Australia and Oceania,[10] which inherits the role of the now-defunct Standing Conference of Canonical Orthodox Churches in Australia. At a first glance, the website of the Assembly gives the impression of co-ordinated efforts between the various jurisdictions in the region. But a genuine co-operation remains a dream, not a fact. Barriers unrelated to the Gospel and the Eastern Orthodox ethos preclude an authentic interaction between jurisdictions. The main difficulty, once again, is the ethnocentric orientation of these jurisdictions, which affects Australian Orthodoxy as much as it does the worldwide Orthodox family, whose profound disunity was apparent on the occasion of the Holy and Great Council of 2016.

Jurisdictional disunity and the lack of contextualisation betray a common cause, the absence of synodality. Within jurisdictions, this deficiency takes the form of a gulf between leadership and membership. The two classes nurture different if not opposite aspirations. Whereas the leaders largely observe the ethnic agendas of their headquarters, behaving as though forever migrants,[11] the grassroots, particularly Australian-born members and converts, are interested in bridging their identities, Orthodox and Australian. Challenged by the tensions pertaining to their minority status Down Under, members

---

10. See the website <http://www.orthodox.net.au/en/episcopal-assembly>. Accessed 6 May 2018.
11. See 'Christianity—Orthodox,' ABC Religion & Ethics blog, 2014, available at <http://www.abc.net.au/religion/stories/s817554.htm>. Accessed 6 May 2018.

are interested in shaping an Australian Orthodoxy, rather than per-
petuating nationalist interests foreign to their everyday experience.
The same goes for the rapport between jurisdictions, which show no
interest in pastoral and missionary co-operation. Unfortunately, triumphalism and the rigid hierarchical nature of the Eastern Orthodox jurisdictions represented in Australia and, with few exceptions,
worldwide, make honest conversation over these matters impossible.
It is this that makes me highlight the significance of the Lutheran–
Roman Catholic document under consideration, which contains lessons to be appropriated by the Eastern Orthodox diaspora.

Wisdom from the document

Turning to the matter of what Eastern Orthodox diaspora could learn
from *The Ministry of Oversight*, it is noteworthy that the difficulty
central to the document under consideration, namely, the imbalance between hierarchy and synodality, is common to contemporary
Orthodox experience. But where *The Ministry of Oversight* addresses
the imbalance mainly from an ecclesiological viewpoint, for the
Orthodox diaspora this is a matter of survival.

The Eastern Orthodox represent themselves as ecclesial and synodal, thus communal and consultative. But numerous cracks in the
wall of this narrative have become publicly obvious before and since
the Holy and Great Council of 2016. We have seen above that the
Orthodox inability to synodise internationally or walk together on
the path is symptomatic of a deeper issue: their lack of synodality
at regional or diocesan levels, particularly in the diaspora. Region-
ally, being concerned with ethnic idiosyncrasies and content to define
themselves as migrant communities, the Eastern Orthodox jurisdictions coexisting within one place do not share in each other's life, do
not contextualise their message, and seem incapable of recognising
shared values beyond their cultural differences. At a diocesan level,
everything functions primarily top down, hierarchically, leaving no
room for ecclesial consultation. Although there are exceptions to this
pseudomorphosis, this does not mean that the problem does not exist.

Should it be disposed to listen in the Spirit to the wisdom of other
Christians, Eastern Orthodox diaspora could learn immensely from
the document considered here—most significantly how to balance
hierarchy through fellowship of communion and the ecclesial practice

of synodality. The retrieval of synodality is a matter of urgency both within jurisdictions and between them. The Lutheran–Roman Catholic agreement on the synodal dimension of episcopal ministry reminds the Eastern Orthodox that episcopal ministry cannot function above, outside, and without the Church. The current top down structure of the Orthodox jurisdictions in the diaspora has led to pastoral and missional impasses which threaten their very survival past this generation. The inability of at least some of these jurisdictions to recognise that they are no longer migrant Churches and that they have a duty towards their local constituencies, cannot be overcome without balancing the top down hierarchical figure with a bottom up, synodal approach. This would entail the practice of consultation and fellowship within the jurisdictions and between them.

I end by emphasising once again that among the strengths of the team which wrote *The Ministry of Oversight* are their realistic examination of the facts, ecclesial discernment, and genuine desire for dialogue. If they were considered seriously, the processes these people followed and the document they have produced, particularly the articles discussed above, could remind the Eastern Orthodox diaspora of long-forgotten ecclesial structures. Learning from this document what it means to listen to one another, in order to identify what really matters, may inspire a way back to normality. To survive and thrive in these testing times for Christianity, the Eastern Orthodox diaspora must retrieve the normality of assessing all matters of importance together, returning to a genuine, applied synodality.

Bibliography

Angold, Michael, editor, *The Cambridge History of Christianity*, volume 5, *Eastern Christianity* (Cambridge University Press, 2006).

Bowling, Mark, 'Brisbane Archbishop calls for first synod for entire Catholic Church in Australia since 1937'. <http://catholicleader.com.au/news/brisbane-archbishop-calls-for-first-synod-for-entire-catholic-church-in-australia-since-1937>. Accessed 6 May 2018.

'Christianity—Orthodox'. ABC Religion & Ethics blog, 2014. <http://www.abc.net.au/religion/stories/s817554.htm>. Accessed 6 May 2018.

Costache, Doru, 'Notes on *The Ministry of Oversight* Document.' Text available at <https://www.academia.edu/1467374/Notes_on_The_Ministry_of_Oversight_Document>. Accessed 6 May 2018.

The Assembly of Canonical Orthodox Bishops of Australia and Oceania. < http://www.orthodox.net.au/en/episcopal-assembly>. Accessed 6 May 2018.

Lutheran Church of Australia. 'Office of the Bishop'. <http://www.lca.org.au/departments/office-bishop/>. Accessed 6 May 2018.

Lutheran–Roman Catholic Dialogue in Australia. *The Ministry of Oversight: The Office of Bishop and President in the Church*. Text available at <http://www.cam.org.au/Portals/66/Resources/Documents/LutheranChurch/Ministry_of_Oversight2007.pdf>. Accessed 6 May 2018.

Parry, Ken, editor, *The Blackwell Companion to Eastern Christianity* (Malden, Oxford, Carlton: Blackwell Publishing, 2007).

The Holy and Great Council of the Orthodox Church. <https://www.holycouncil.org/>. Accessed 6 May 2018.

Nurturing and Nourishing a Receptive Disposition Through Process

Geraldine Hawkes

Encounter, conversation and learning are the key elements which shape gatherings hosted by the South Australian Council of Churches (SACC). Our meetings are designed to encourage a receptive disposition by making time for sharing insights around the key questions, 'What is the gift my church needs, seeks, or has received, from another?', 'What does my Church yearn for from another?', and 'Where have we experienced the light of Christ?'.

The stories people tell naturally meander, yet in each story something is revealed of a yearning to be more, a desire for wholeness, embracing the fragility of their own church, in whatever arena, and opening ourselves to the beauty and truth that is manifest in another.

Such disposition is further nurtured through the frequent presentation and development of a range of resources which act as preludes to walking the way of Receptive Ecumenism.

This paper describes and reflects on three processes that SACC has developed and which have been used across the churches in SA and further afield: *Receptive Ecumenism: Gifts of Healing, Reimagining Women's Participation in the Church through Receptive Ecumenism,* and *Reimagining our Unity in Christ through Receptive Ecumenism.*

In the ten years since first introducing the Member Churches[1] to Receptive Ecumenism, SACC has witnessed church councils, com-

---

1. Members of the South Australian Council of Churches: Anglican Church of Australia—Diocese of Adelaide and Diocese of Willochra; Catholic Archdiocese of Adelaide and Catholic Diocese of Port Pirie; Churches of Christ in South Australia and Northern Territory; Coptic Orthodox Church—Diocese of Melbourne and Affiliated Regions; Greek Orthodox Archdiocese of Australia— Third Archdiocesan District of South Australia and Northern Territory; Lutheran

mittees, synods and dioceses across South Australia (SA) gradually and incrementally becoming more fully imbued with and attracted by the approach that Receptive Ecumenism offers.

It is clear is that in order to enter into this space of receptivity there has to be an easing of traditional ways of discussing and engaging with denominational life and mission, within denominations as well as across, and a willingness to take on new ways. Especially important for this change to happen is disposition. How one denomination perceives itself alongside another can either help or hinder its willingness to recognise Receptive Ecumenism as a pathway that has the potential to lead to a more authentic institutional manifestation of unity in the Way of Christ. One way that SACC has approached this need for a new disposition both towards self and towards the other is through attention to process, on the basis that process and disposition accompany and support one another.

Following the 2012 visit to Australia and New Zealand of Paul Murray, Professor of Systematic Theology at Durham University, and initiator of Receptive Ecumenism, SACC prepared the resource handbook *Healing Gifts for Wounded Hands: The promise and potential of Receptive Ecumenism.*[2] The handbook, which has been taken up and promoted by a number bodies, including the Anglican Centre in Rome, Churches Together in England and the Centre for Catholic Studies at Durham University, offers a practical introduction to Receptive Ecumenism. It also includes four Activities which can be used by any church council or committee (*Ecclesial Examination of Conscience*—discerning the need for healing; *Receiving the Gift of the Other*—naming the gifts in different denominations; The *Curiosity Box*—eliciting a spirit of enquiry and learning; *Signposts*—our major strengths may have a flipside weakness)[3] .

SACC has also developed, facilitated and offered workshops, conversations, presentations, lectures, and guidance for inter-church

Church of Australia—South Australia-Northern Territory District; Religious Society of Friends South Australia and Northern Territory Regional Meeting; Romanian Orthodox Episcopate of Australia/New Zealand—South Australia Parish; Salvation Army South Australia Division; St Urael Ethiopian Orthodox Tewahdo Church in South Australia Inc; Uniting Church in South Australia.

2. It can be downloaded from the SACC website: <http://www.sacc.asn.au>. Accessed 8 October 2018.

3. Please see: <http://www.sacc.asn.au>. Accessed 8 October 2018.

councils, national church bodies, theological colleges, heads of churches, parish councils and ecumenical conferences. Whether SACC initiated these or was invited to develop and deliver them, it has always been done in partnership with others, and in response to their expressed context and need.

The possibility of acting in all these ways has been made possible by the clear commitment of the General Council of SACC to Receptive Ecumenism and the employment of an Ecumenical Facilitator to guide, develop and support engagement with the way of Receptive Ecumenism.

Process I: Receptive Ecumenism: Gifts of Healing

Receptive Ecumenism: Gifts of Healing, was a pilot project initiated by SACC and held over a period of three months in 2013. It involved two groups of people with a deep connection and commitment to SACC and a familiarity with and curiosity about Receptive Ecumenism—the Anglican Ecumenical Network (AEN) and the (Catholic) Diocesan Ecumenical and Interfaith Commission (DEIC). Each has denominational responsibility for ecumenism, with around ten members each.

The primary aims of the project were to learn more about processes that would be helpful, or unhelpful, for the application of Receptive Ecumenism, and to draw the participants into a new disposition towards one another. An unarticulated hope was that through the experience, participants would find ways to encourage others in their denomination to adopt the methodology of Receptive Ecumenism.

Members of each body had for some time been exploring ways to connect with one another and to share insights about how they were responding to their remit for ecumenism. The invitation to participate in this project offered them a practical avenue for building the relationship as well as providing an approach that encouraged listening and learning rather than the usual 'telling about'.

For the purpose of this article, I will describe the project from the DEIC position only. The DEIC first hosted the AEN participants who reciprocated this hospitality at a later date. There were three distinct steps or Conversations:

Conversation #1 Listening to the Spirit—Discernment

The first step for DEIC was to name what aspect it considered it needed to learn from the wisdom and practice of the local Anglican Church. Whatever aspect was identified would then form the topic for DEIC's listening to and learning from AEN. At one of its regular meetings, DEIC considered: *Where in our structure or practice or systems are we lacking, or hurting, or weakened—and therefore not reflecting fully the light of Christ?*

Generally, the identification of a 'learning' question would emerge from a longer process of prayerful discernment, seeking the guidance of the Spirit. For the purposes of this project, it was agreed simply to find a question about which DEIC was curious, which was to some extent within their sphere of responsibility and which would be within AEN's capacity to respond.

Eventually, they decided that they wished to learn more about collaborative decision-making, which the Catholic Archdiocese was engaged in developing throughout its structures and systems.

DEIC then contacted AEN and invited them to meet at a mutually agreed time over prayer and hospitality to describe to DEIC 'the practice and experience of collaborative decision-making in the local Anglican Church'.

Conversation #2 Listening to the Other

At this second conversation, lasting just under two hours, DEIC hosted AEN. There was no formal agenda, no phones, no distractions. There was cake, coffee and conversation, and an atmosphere of ease in the room. People chatted, and after a while, the cups and plates were set aside, and people took their seats in the circle for a time of shared prayer and then stories.

There were six present from each body, and I attended as a listening and learning facilitator. One by one, each member of AEN described the practice of collaborative decision-making. Six stories were shared, from a bishop, a deacon, three laypersons and a priest.

- Anglican Synodical Process and Diocesan Structures
- Parish Councils and the relative powers of clergy
- On being a Church Warden and Parish Councillor

- Parish sharing through informal Open Forum Discussions
- Synod's Westminster System of Governance
- The Nomination Process for Clergy Appointments

This segment took over an hour and was both expansive and yet focused. During this time, DEIC listened and only asked questions for clarification. When AEN was finished, a prayer for peace was shared before people departed.

AEN later shared their reflections on the gathering and comments emerged along the following lines:

- The gathering immediately felt so welcoming, receptive and hospitable
- They liked beginning with light refreshments and conversation
- Catholic members listened extremely attentively and enthusiastically
- The opportunity to share both positive and negative experiences of Anglican decision making felt well received, and any vulnerabilities were really embraced
- It was truly an experience of being on holy ground together and an amazing privilege to speak openly and to be heard so generously
- It felt good to be Anglican.

Conversation #3 Receiving Gifts of Healing

The final step involved DEIC at its next scheduled meeting reflecting on what, if any, was the gift that DEIC heard from what AEN shared, and what might this gift mean for DEIC.

Comments included:

- There was much richness both in the process and in the content.
- Some of what they heard was quite new and engendered curiosity and inspiration about how voices 'on the edge', the voices of the whole people of God, contribute to the life and mission of the Anglican Church.
- There was a particular interest in relation to procedures and structures around Synod, clergy appointments and the role of church warden.

Project Conclusions

Ideally, more time would have been allocated to the reflection by DEIC on the second conversation, and any steps would have been identified for integration into the work of the DEIC or the Archdiocese. However, each of the areas identified merited, at least, communication to others in the Archdiocese who had such responsibility or interest.

From comments received from participants, and the stance of people during each stage, it seemed that the processes around the preparation and at the gathering elicited and engendered a disposition of humility, openness, listening and receptivity.

At another time AEN replicated the process, with a different question, and DEIC were hosted in the same manner, and with the same richness of appreciation expressed by AEN for the wisdom residing in the Catholic experience that may in time help further shape and inform what it means to be Anglican.

Process II: Reimagining Women's Participation in the Church through Receptive Ecumenism

This process was developed in response to a request to SACC from the Australian Catholic Theological Association (ACTA) to assist in developing a plenary session entitled 'Reimagining Women's Participation in the Church through Receptive Ecumenism', to be held at the Annual Conference of ACTA in Melbourne, Australia, in July 2016.

The reason for choosing the method of Receptive Ecumenism was the recognition that in being open to listening, both to ecumenical friends and the Spirit, new insights, creativity, imagination and learning might emerge on women's participation in the Catholic Church.

A small working group of ACTA members was established prior to the Annual Conference to work with SACC. When we reached agreement on the process both before and during the session, five people—four women and one man (all Catholic)—were invited to take a particular role. It involved each of them meeting with at least one other person from another church (described as their host), and asking them about their experiences and insights on women's participation and roles in their church, especially on an aspect that is flourishing. This would result in having up to five different perspectives on women's participation from across the church in Australia.

Each ACTA person was to arrange a time to meet with their host and to listen to what they had to say without judgment or comment, other than to ask questions of clarification. Of particular interest was the description of any theological or scriptural basis for practice or structures in the host church.

In addition, all members of ACTA were invited to do likewise, and an outline was made available to them as a guide.

Everyone who had met with someone was encouraged in the ensuing days to reflect on what they had heard:

- To whom did you listen and from which church?
- How did you feel as you listened?
- From what you heard, describe the gift you received—something that caught your imagination, or was new or illuminating, and which you consider may have the potential to lead towards conversion or reform within a process, practice, system or structure in any part of the church. Might it inform or illuminate my experience?

On the day of the conference plenary, following morning tea, the five people who had been specifically invited to prepare took their seats together with the SACC Ecumenical Facilitator. We sat in a small circle, around which sat other members of ACTA in a rather haphazard circle due to the large number of people (around forty to fifty perhaps). The purpose of the seating arrangement was to foster a conversational and collegial atmosphere, rather than one of delivery or of distance.

Each of the five described their encounter—with whom they had met (Lutherans, Anglicans, Uniting and the Church of Sweden), what they had heard, how they felt, what had sparked their imagination— for about five to ten minutes (since there was a conference timetable to which all had to adhere, and we had ninety minutes total available). The process allowed for other stories to be shared, and for questions of clarification to be interspersed throughout.

Others from ACTA can describe the impact of the discoveries on the topic they had selected and any next steps. What was of particular interest to SACC and to me as facilitator were the comments from the five people: all had appreciated the opportunity to listen to another; each had received new insights and hope for further possibilities about women's participation; some had been surprised by the feelings of gentle vulnerability and of humility that had emanated from participation; others spoke of relationships being strengthened and a new understanding and respect of the other. While one or two ACTA members expressed some reservation about the relevance of the process in such forums, most ACTA members commented that they had found the process as a whole to have been both moving and significant.

Process III: Reimagining our Unity in Christ through Receptive Ecumenism

The third process was largely similar to that of ACTA. The audience this time was SACC Member Churches, and a date was set for a learning event to be held in Adelaide in July 2017.

The focus question was, 'What might my Church learn from your Church about welcoming newcomers, nurturing hospitality and nourishing an active congregation?'.

Four people from four different denominations—Catholic, Coptic Orthodox, Greek Orthodox and Uniting—accepted SACC's invitation to share this 'learning question' with a group from another denomination.

Six weeks before the gathering the five of us met and over a light meal provided by one of the four. We discussed how each would approach another church and any reservations or concerns that they had.

In the intervening weeks, each made contact with a range of denominations, including Anglican, Salvation Army, Catholic and Uniting. Having listened without judgment or comment, there was encouragement to be attentive to any theological or scriptural insights.

The four were also encouraged to reflect on their feelings as well as on their insights in the days following the encounter with their host.

The July date arrived for the sharing of the stories, and two and a half hours had been set aside. As people arrived, they enjoyed morning tea, and after a time they stopped, and prayer was led by the convenor of one of SACC's committees. Twenty-two people from seven different denominations were present, together with SACC's Ecumenical Facilitator.

The seating arrangement and process for learning about welcoming, hospitality and nourishing an active community was in the round, similar to ACTA's.

The four pre-invited people from different denominations had about five minutes each to share what they had heard, with five minutes to respond to any questions or comments.

Three other people who were present had also followed the process out of personal interest, and time was given to listen to what they had heard.

The final part of the session involved listening to a Gospel, randomly selected and read by one person, followed by the question for all to ponder: How does this text influence my understanding of the experience?.

At the end of the session, many in the gathering commented that they had each discovered something new about welcoming and hospitality to take back to their parish or synod or council. The Gospel passage had also shed helpful light on their consideration and would form a basis for ongoing reflection.

Before departing everyone was invited to reflect in silence on the process. Then some spoke of the morning's listening as having been moving and significant, that an amazing breadth of wisdom had been shared that was respectful of story, and had opened them to deeper discovery and learning, and enriched their understanding of Receptive Ecumenism.

Concluding Reflections on the Processes

All who took an active role in these three processes were able to describe new insights. How such insights would be integrated authentically within a denomination is another question. What was of particular interest to SACC was whether the processes that were used would nurture a receptive disposition and lead people into a meaningful engagement with Receptive Ecumenism with its potential to draw all into a deeper encounter with Christ.

From feedback following each process described in this article and from being deeply involved at every stage, the abiding memory is one of tenderness; a tenderness that was both strong and gentle, that evoked possibility and receptivity, and embraced humility and vulnerability. Postures and feelings of smugness and competitiveness seemed to slip away, and be replaced by graciousness, generosity and a deep and loving delight in the other. The importance of relationships was named again and again, and the listening to and sharing of stories was described as like being on holy ground.

The processes outlined in this essay continue to evolve through practice and reflective conversations and are available at SACC's website[4]. SACC hopes that they will assist people, whatever their Church context, to develop further a disposition, towards one another and towards the Spirit, of listening, learning and loving in the Way of Christ.

---

4.   Please see: <http://www.sacc.asn.au>, accessed 8 October 2018.

A Forum for Theology in the World Vol 5 No 2/2018

Receptive Ecumenism, Ecumenical Learning and Learning Communities

John Littleton

This paper explores the possibilities of linking the approach of Receptive Ecumenism with learning community strategies to enhance ecumenical learning within and between learning communities. After a general description of the numerous contexts in which learning community processes are used, the paper explores findings from various scholars and research projects on learning processes in church communities. The paper concludes with examples from my own context, which illustrate how these various research findings point to ways the practice of Receptive Ecumenism might enhance ecumenical learning outcomes in faith community contexts.

The approach of Receptive Ecumenism

'The question Receptive Ecumenism asks is: what can we—and what do we need to—learn and receive, with integrity, from the other traditions?'[1] The importance of that question cannot be overstated. It defines the approach of Receptive Ecumenism as listening to and learning from the other, rather than telling the other.

Paul Murray writes that Receptive Ecumenism provides an appropriate organising principle for contemporary ecumenism.

> This is the principle that considerable further progress is indeed possible, but only if each of the traditions, both singly

---

1. South Australian Council of Churches, *Healing Gifts for Wounded Hands: The Promise and Potential of Receptive Ecumenism.* 1, at <http://www.sacc.asn.au/_data/Healing_Gifts_for_Wounded_Hands_May_2014.pdf>, Accessed 25 March 2018.

and jointly, make a clear, programmatic shift from prioritising the question 'What do our various others first need to learn from us?' to asking instead, 'What is it that we need to learn and can learn, or receive, with integrity from our others?'[2]

Learning community strategies provide processes which can be used together with a Receptive Ecumenism approach to enhance ecumenical learning outcomes.

Ecumenical Learning

In 1989 the World Council of Churches (WCC) published definitions of ecumenical learning. Two of these are:

1. Learning which enables people, while remaining rooted in one tradition of the church, to become open and responsive to the richness and perspective of other churches, so that they become more active in seeking unity, openness and collaboration between churches.

2. Ecumenical learning is a process by which:
   - diverse groups and individuals
   - well-rooted in their own faith, traditions, cultures and contexts
   - are enabled to risk honest encounters with one another before God
   - as they study and struggle together in community
   - with personally relevant issues
   - in light of the scriptures, the traditions of their faith, worship and global realities
   - resulting in communal action in faithfulness to God's intention for the unity of the church and humankind, and for justice, peace, and the integrity of creation.[3]

Both of these WCC definitions focus on process rather than content—the importance of the learning processes through which the ecumenical learning outcomes emerge. The definitions represent a

---

2. Paul Murray, 'Introducing Receptive Ecumenism', in *The Ecumenist, a Journal of Theology, Culture and Society*, 51/2 (2014): 1.
3. World Council of Churches (WCC), *Alive Together: A Practical Guide To Ecumenical Learning* (Geneva, Switzerland: Sub-Unit on Education, World Council of Churches, 1989), 7–8.

learning process and learner-centred emphasis, rather than a teacher and content-centred emphasis for ecumenical education. And they go further than just process. They also point to learning outcomes—acknowledging, identifying and stating the learning that has happened for learners—and then go on to measurable outcomes: the participants' thoughts and feelings; their knowledge, understanding and practice of the Christian faith; and an appreciation of the attitudes and behaviours of others.

This is analogous to current understandings of a parish or congregation as a learning community, with its special learning processes (holistic, collaborative and reflective) for undertaking learning on whatever topic. A learning community approach is also process-centred. Process is as important as content.

In his book *Creative Ecumenical Education*, Simon Oxley referred to the WCC's definitions of ecumenical learning and identified the connection between ecumenical learning and learning communities.[4] He wanted to help churches to become learning communities. Oxley discussed a number of educational processes that facilitated ecumenical learning, including: encounter with the 'other', learning from the Bible and through worship, critical thinking, participatory learning, communal learning and creating safe spaces for learning. He noted that ecumenical education involved congregational as well as individual learning. The educational processes mentioned by Oxley describe some of the shared understandings that exist within the literature on the parish as a learning community.

These shared understandings are ripe with possibilities for expanding the community learning model from a parish arena to an ecumenical arena, and, I would argue, most rewardingly through a Receptive Ecumenical framework. The profound benefit of these shared understandings is that we come to see the gathered people as the primary setting and the formative influence for a holistic approach to faith education. Such a community should strive to create hospitable, safe learning spaces, where each person is valued, their gifts recognised and their contribution encouraged. All members of the learning community should seek to help each other to become

---

4. Simon Oxley, *Creative Ecumenical Education: Learning from One Another* (Geneva: Risk Book Series, World Council of Churches Publications, 2002), 12–13, 44–45, 88–89, 125–126.

life-long, life-wide and life-deep learners. Leadership needs to be biblically literate, reflective, shared, consultative, collaborative and encouraging. All of this can lead to learning communities which are capable of self-reflection, self-criticism, innovation and creation of new futures in changing times.[5]

Oxley emphasised that to take ecumenical education seriously 'we must work to help churches become learning communities rather than domesticating communities—to have a broad or multiple perspective rather than a single, narrow view of their faith and the world'.[6] But does research support the validity of Oxley's contention, by showing that a learning community approach benefits ecumenical learning outcomes? This article argues that it does, and that a Receptive Ecumenism approach together with learning community processes can enhance ecumenical processes and outcomes.

Learning Community Approaches Contextualised in Parishes

Learning communities are formed in various contexts: in schools, higher education, business or community organisations, churches, and in online and e-learning situations. The learning community concept is customised for and defined in a variety of contexts.

Research conducted in those contexts shows evidence of the positive impact of learning community processes on the learning outcomes of students, on their achievement and involvement, as well as improved learning outcomes for teachers and educational institutions.[7] In school and higher education contexts, the use of learning community approaches impacts significantly on learning outcomes.

---

5. Twelve shared understandings about the characteristics of learning communities in parishes are spelled out in greater detail in John Littleton, *Enhance Learning in Parishes: A Learning Community Approach for Church Congregations* (Adelaide: MediaCom Education Inc, 2017), 24–25.

6. Oxley, *Creative Ecumenical Education*, 44.

7. Milton Cox, 'A Journey in Scholarship Development: The Role of Learning Communities—A Message from the Editor-in-Chief', in *Learning Communities Journal*, 1/1 (2009): 1–5; Littleton, *Enhance Learning in Parishes*, 10; Susanne Mary Owen, 'Teacher professional learning communities in innovative contexts: "ah hah moments", "passion" and "making a difference" for student learning', in *Professional Development in Education Journal*, 41/1(2015): 57–74.

In parish contexts a number of learning community approaches have been used, including the work of Norma Cook Everist, Barbara Fleischer and my own approach. These approaches are based on an understanding that the whole life of a parish is the focus for education in the Christian faith. Educators appreciate that a learning component resides in every aspect of a parish's life. Research conducted in parish contexts has shown evidence of the positive effect of learning community processes on faith learning outcomes of parishioners.

Writing from the Lutheran tradition, Everist has explored the topic in *The Church as Learning Community*.[8] The purpose of her book was to present a vision of the whole parish as learning community and to provide a guide for religious educators as they helped congregations to become learning communities. Everist included the gathered Sunday church experience and the daily and weekly arenas of life in her understanding of a learning community.

Fleischer conducted research in a Roman Catholic parish in New Orleans, USA. Through this case study of forty-six lay pastoral ministry leaders in a parish, Fleischer concluded that involvement in ministry, which included reflection on that ministry practice, was ' . . . a major pathway for learning in a congregation . . . For both the Pastoral Team members and the Ministry Team Leaders, involvement in ministry was a major pathway for their own learning, both for personal faith development and for moving toward a shared ministerial vision'.[9] This example illustrated that, in the context of a collaborative, reflective and ministerially active parish, leaders and parishioners, through team ministry, grew in their faith.

The outcomes in these various contexts accord with those of my own doctoral research project on a learning community approach in parishes in Australia by demonstrating a positive association between learning community approaches and learning outcomes.

---

8. Norma Cook Everist, *The Church as Learning Community: A Comprehensive Guide to Christian Education* (Nashville, USA: Abingdon Press, 2002), 10–11.
9. Barbara J Fleischer, 'The Ministering Community as Context for Religious Education: A Case Study of St. Gabriel's Catholic Parish', in *Religious Education*, 101/1 (2006): 104, 120. An introduction to more literature on the parish as a learning community is available in Littleton, *Enhance Learning in Parishes*, 21–33.

Learning Community Approach in Parishes Researched

The learning processes described by the WCC, Oxley and given in the accounts of other educational contexts, relate to the findings of my doctoral research on the enhancement of learning in forty-seven parishes within the Anglican Diocese of Adelaide, South Australia. This research examined parish educational ministry through the lens of a learning community approach. For the purposes of that project, I defined a learning community in the parish context as 'a visionary community of faith where leaders and members, while respecting a diversity of abilities and perspectives, practise holistic, collaborative and theologically reflective learning processes'.[10]

In that study, I demonstrate that the learning community processes—of holism, collaboration and theological reflection—when intentionally practised in parishes, enhance learning outcomes in terms of the knowledge, understanding and practice of the Christian faith in and through Jesus Christ.

Holistic processes are present where there is a shared vision of the whole parish which combines the five avenues of parish learning available in an Anglican parish structure: individual learning; group learning; congregational learning; community engagement learning; and dialogical learning. The degree of holism depends upon the extent to which all five parts of parish learning figure in the profile of parish life.

Collaborative processes in parishes involve people in the sharing of leadership within the ministry and outreach responsibilities of the parish. Members work and learn together interactively, enjoying and respecting the abilities and contributions of others in achieving a common task. The degree to which learning processes are collaborative depends on the widespread sharing of leadership and the regular use of teamwork, the gifts and skills of parishioners, and the extent of consultation and networking.

Theologically reflective processes in parishes involve people in reflecting upon or thinking about their present life actions in the light of the biblical story and traditions, and then moving forward, renewed for future action. The degree to which learning processes are reflective is indicated by the extent to which the leadership, the sermons, the worship services, the parish groups, the decision-making

---

10. Littleton, *Enhance Learning in Parishes*, 13.

of the parish and the membership show evidence of some form of theological reflection.

Parish survey and focus group results revealed a spectrum of responses from across the parishes in the Diocese. The research showed a moderate, positive and clear association between these three learning community processes and learning outcomes.

Disciples learn. Learning is a change in attitude and behaviour by a person or group of people. As defined for the research project:

> Faith learning is a process of growing in the knowledge, understanding and practice of the Christian faith in and through Jesus Christ. By growth in faith learning, I mean the degree to which people report that their knowledge, understanding and practice of the Christian faith have grown or been enhanced.[11]

The research findings revealed a definite trend.

> The general trend across the spectrum of parishes indicated that the greater the presence of these learning community processes in a parish, the greater the likelihood that there would be much growth and enhancement in faith learning, with a lesser presence of these processes tending to correlate with less growth and enhancement in faith learning.[12]

Learning through conversation and participation was highlighted in the research project. In parishes with enhanced faith learning, research participants reported that they learnt through conversation, participation in teams and in the sharing of ministry tasks. The focus group findings confirmed the survey findings and placed an emphasis upon collaborative and interactive faith learning. These findings can also apply to ecumenical learning processes and outcomes. Conversation and participation across church communities provide opportunities for that learning. Much growth in ecumenical learning outcomes is a likely trend when holistic, collaborative and theological reflective learning processes are used in the practice of Receptive Ecumenism in faith community contexts.

---

11. Littleton, *Enhance Learning in Parishes*, 49.
12. Littleton, *Enhance Learning in Parishes*, 68.

Further, the finding that faith learning happened through conversation with others is consistent with the findings from a Receptive Ecumenism research project conducted in England. Helen Savage's empirical research study about 'Ordinary Learning' was based on a Receptive Ecumenism survey of adult learning and formation groups in northeast England between 2009 and 2011; research sponsored by Durham University. Groups from fifty-one localities participated in the study, involving groups from Anglican, Baptist, Methodist, Roman Catholic, Salvation Army and United Reformed Churches. Evidence also came from one wholly ecumenical group. Savage's research findings 'found that, in the context of church learning groups, ordinary learning is founded on conversation and the quality of relationships'.[13] Participants valued the opportunity to share their experiences, listen to the stories of others in an atmosphere of trust, acceptance and mutual respect. Conversation and quality relationships are important for much growth in learning outcomes during Receptive Ecumenism activities.

The Practice of Receptive Ecumenism in the local context

A Receptive Ecumenism approach involves listening to and learning from the other in Christ. A learning community approach helps people to be receptive; to enter and engage with a listening, learning and reflective disposition in a safe place.

Four practical examples illustrate the local application in Adelaide of an ecumenical learning community methodology informed by Receptive Ecumenism: a lecture, an ecumenical conversation, a pilgrimage and a fishbowl technique. In each example the three learning community processes of holism, collaboration and theological reflection were used in a number of ways and influenced the choice of appropriate methods. A Receptive Ecumenism approach, combined with these learning community processes, enabled ecumenical learning outcomes to emerge through discernment in the Spirit of Christ.

---

13. Helen Savage, 'Ordinary Learning', in *Exploring Ordinary Theology: Everyday Christian Believing and the Church*, edited by Jeff Astley and Leslie Francis (Surrey UK: Ashgate, 2013), 199–201. On page 1, Astley defines ordinary theology as 'the theological beliefs and processes of believing that find expression in the reflective God-talk of those believers who have received no scholarly theological education'.

A lecture

In Adelaide, for a number of years from 2008, the South Australian Council of Churches Committee for Ecumenical Learning organised an annual lecture on an ecumenical theme using a participatory approach. Two responders who had prior access to the text of the lecture followed on from the lecture presentation (twenty to thirty minutes) by the guest speaker. Each responder spoke for about five to ten minutes. Then, all participants discussed the topic for about ten minutes in small groups of three to five people. Questions or comments to the guest speaker and others concluded the ninety-minute session. By the end of this process the sixty to eighty people present had become a community of learning.

An ecumenical conversation

In 2016, members of the Ecumenical Network for the Anglican Diocese of Adelaide decided to change the format of their gatherings. Instead of a meeting format an ecumenical conversation is now held based on a presentation and a shared reflection on the topic (there is minimal note taking on necessary business). In conclusion a personal or group reflection is offered in response to questions like: What have I learned? What will I do differently? What biblical passage comes to mind? Are there any steps I can take within my sphere of influence, someone to speak to, some action to undertake? Ecumenical learning outcomes are articulated through a reflective process.[14]

A pilgrimage

In April 2017, members celebrated the seventieth birthday of the South Australian Council of Churches (SACC) under the Theme: 'An Exchange of Gifts on the Journey towards Unity'. The events took place in the city of Adelaide on a Saturday from 10.00am until 3.30pm, with over a hundred people participating. The organisers had invited the communities of four city churches—Pilgrim (Uniting), St Francis Xavier (Roman Catholic), St Mary Magdalene's (Anglican) and St Ste-

---

14. Other practical resources are available in the booklet *Healing Gifts for Wounded Hands*. A workshop format on 'Receiving the Gift of the Other' is included as Activity 2, 4–6.

phen's (Lutheran)—to host a pilgrimage to enable the SACC General Council members and people from across the churches to gather and celebrate these seventy years. This Pilgrimage experience of walking, conversing, eating, reading the Bible and worshipping together was impressive, positive and inspirationally grounded in a recognition of the Presence of Christ evident amongst the participants and in all the Churches visited.

A fishbowl technique

In July 2017, the SACC held an event in a parish entitled 'Exchange of Gifts: Reimagining our Unity in Christ through Receptive Ecumenism', using a fishbowl technique. The interactive conversation amongst the twenty-one participants from a wide variety of churches focussed on the learning question: 'How does your Church welcome newcomers, nurture hospitality and nourish an active congregation?' Four responders (from the Coptic Orthodox Church, the Uniting Church, the Roman Catholic Church and the Greek Orthodox Church) opened the conversation by sharing what they had discovered through the learning question from listening to answers that people from other churches gave prior to the event. Other participants then entered the conversation, which gradually moved through information and content learning towards deep ecumenical learning outcomes about hospitality, welcoming, and growing an active congregation, with the potential to draw a part of their own church more fully into the way of Christ.

These four examples serve as evidence of the multiple ways in which a Receptive Ecumenism approach using learning community processes can be applied in varying contexts to enrich learning outcomes.[15]

---

15. Caution may need to be exercised about the transferability and generalisability of the research findings about parishes in the Anglican Diocese of Adelaide. Nevertheless, the findings provide helpful insights and are consistent with other learning community research studies in a variety of contexts. The short-term intention on each occasion mentioned, for example, a pilgrimage or a fishbowl event, is for the leadership to help participants become a community of learning or a learning community in that situation at that time. In the longer term, helping churches to become learning communities is a way forward for Receptive Ecumenism.

Conclusion

This paper has considered the benefits for ecumenical learning outcomes when Receptive Ecumenism and learning community processes come together. Examples of this in local faith community contexts have illustrated ways in which learning outcomes were enhanced. The paper has thus shown that a Receptive Ecumenism approach together with learning community strategies leads to deeper ecumenical outcomes in church and inter-church activities.

Bibliography

Astley, Jeff and Leslie J Francis, editors, *Exploring Ordinary Theology: Everyday Christian Believing and the Church* (Surrey UK: Ashgate, 2013).

Cox, Milton, 'A Journey in Scholarship Development: The Role of Learning Communities—A Message from the Editor-in-Chief', in *Learning Communities Journal*, 1/1 (2009): 1–5.

Everist, Norma Cook, *The Church as Learning Community: A Comprehensive Guide to Christian Education* (Nashville, USA: Abingdon Press, 2002).

Fleischer, Barbara J, 'The Ministering Community as Context for Religious Education: A Case Study of St Gabriel's Catholic Parish', in *Religious Education,* 101/1 (2006): 104–22.

Littleton, John, *Enhance Learning in Parishes: A Learning Community Approach for Church Congregations* (Adelaide: MediaCom Education Inc, 2017).

Murray, Paul, 'Introducing Receptive Ecumenism', in *The Ecumenist, a Journal of Theology, Culture and Society*, 51/2 (2014): 1–8.

Owen, Susanne Mary, 'Teacher Professional Learning Communities in Innovative Contexts: "ah hah moments", "passion" and "making a difference" for Student Learning', in *Professional Development in Education Journal*, 41/1(2015), 57–74.

Oxley, Simon, *Creative Ecumenical Education: Learning from One Another* (Geneva: Risk Book Series, World Council of Churches Publications, 2002).

Savage, Helen, 'Ordinary Learning', in *Exploring Ordinary Theology: Everyday Christian Believing and the Church*, edited by Jeff Astley and Leslie Francis (Surrey UK: Ashgate, 2013), 199–208.

South Australian Council of Churches, *Healing Gifts for Wounded Hands: The promise and potential of Receptive Ecumenism* 2014 at <http://www.sacc.asn.au/_data/Healing_Gifts_for_Wounded_Hands_May_2014.pdf>, Accessed 25 March 2018.

World Council of Churches, *Alive Together: A Practical Guide to Ecumenical Learning* (Geneva: Sub-Unit on Education, World Council of Churches Publications, 1989).

A Forum for Theology in the World Vol 5 No 2/2018

Receptive Ecumenism: A Pedagogical Process

Sara Gehlin

A Source of Pedagogical Creativity

Receptive ecumenism can be practised in many different ways. Factors like context, timeframe, thematic orientation, and group composition influence the way receptive ecumenism takes shape in practice. Receptive ecumenism inspires pedagogical creativity—it inspires the development of new tools to support ecumenical learning. Its principal question—*What is it that we in our tradition need to learn and receive, with integrity, from others?*—forms the starting point for pedagogical processes which can be designed for different kinds of groups and contexts.

The insights shared in this article come from the experience of leading a pedagogical process inspired by receptive ecumenism.[1] This process, spanning 2016 and 2017, was a step in the establishment of receptive ecumenism in Sweden.[2] It took place within the framework of an ecumenical project initiated by the Workgroup for Mission Theology at the Christian Council of Sweden and the Swedish Mission Council. The project engaged representatives from the four 'church families' recognised by the Christian Council of Sweden: the Orthodox, Catholic, Lutheran, and Free Church families.[3]

---

1. This article is a revised version of the book chapter 'Receptiv ekumenik—en pedagogisk process', which is to be published in a future Swedish study guide on receptive ecumenism.
2. The pedagogical process was conducted in co-operation between Sara Gehlin and Sven-Erik Fjellström.
3. The member churches of the Christian Council of Sweden are defined as four 'church families': the Orthodox (16 member churches), Catholic (1 member church), Lutheran (4 member churches), and Free Church (8 member churches).

The project eventually took the shape of a *Pilgrimage*. Accordingly, the pedagogical choices and actions discussed in this article reflect the work of the Pilgrimage. Leading this Pilgrimage as a pedagogical exercise required discerning and responding to a number of variables which all proved significant: *place and movement, theme, structure, dynamics, challenges, timeframes*, and *goals*. In the following, the influence of each of these variables will be discussed in the light of the Pilgrimage as a pedagogical process.

Place and Movement

As the name indicates, the Pilgrimage involved movement between places. The choice of meeting places was particularly significant to the way receptive ecumenism could happen. The principal question of receptive ecumenism called for consideration of who were to be the guests and who the hosts at a given meeting place. During the Pilgrimage, the constitution of the group was decisive in the choice of meeting places.

The Pilgrimage, which engaged participants from an array of different church traditions, exemplified how receptive ecumenism can be carried out multilaterally, as distinct from other receptive ecumenical projects which have been bilateral, and where meetings only alternated between the two groups' buildings. There are also receptive ecumenical initiatives, which have engaged participants from one single church tradition. Yet even these can imply a movement outwards, where the participants seek to encounter and gain knowledge from representatives of other traditions. In all cases, upon returning to their group, participants exchange ideas and insights on how to deepen one's understanding, and to contribute to the renewal of one's own tradition.[4]

The Pilgrimage had four destinations: four Christian centres which are each key to the life of the Orthodox, Catholic, Lutheran, and Free Church families in Sweden.[5] Along the journey, all partici-

---

4. The examples derive from the work on receptive ecumenism which has been initiated by the International Network of Societies for Catholic Theology, the South Australian Council of Churches, and the Dominican Sisters of Rögle Monastery in Sweden.
5. The participants in the Pilgrimage visited the four centres in the following order: St Ignatios Andliga Akademi (Orthodox) April 2016, Bjärka Säby (Free

pants were both hosts and guests. The meetings took place every six months and were carried out over an afternoon and evening, as well as the morning of the following day.

The Pilgrimage involved taking part in the community life of each of the four meeting places. Participants engaged in the host community's prayer tradition and were provided with meals that were sometimes cooked according to the particular traditions of the host-church family. Thus, the process of receptive ecumenical learning engaged several senses. It was not only about listening, but also about seeing, smelling, and tasting.

When the Pilgrimage was set as a framework for receptive ecumenical work, the World Council of Churches' ongoing program 'Pilgrimage of Justice and Peace' was one source of inspiration. Another was the pilgrim movement, which is central to many church communities in Sweden. The Pilgrimage provided a format for ecumenical learning where the meeting at each new place expanded the visiting participants' horizons.

Theme

We now turn to the particular theme chosen as the learning focus of this Pilgrimage. Receptive ecumenism has proved helpful in facilitating conversations on themes that are often avoided, but which call for further exploration and learning. Receptive ecumenism has enabled conversations on themes that are controversial, but essential to discuss, in order to find new ways of managing difficulties within churches. Hospitality, church structure, women's participation and ministry in churches, the nourishment of an active congregation, conversion, and leadership number among the themes that have so far been addressed through receptive ecumenical processes.[6]

The Pilgrimage also focused on a theme which has caused controversy within and between the churches: the theme of *mission*. Yet the choice of this theme was natural, given that the Pilgrimage devel-

Church) October 2016, Marielund (Catholic) March 2017, Stiftsgården i Rättvik (Lutheran) September 2017.

6. These thematic examples are drawn from the work on receptive ecumenism which has been carried out at the initiative of the Centre for Catholic Studies at Durham University in the UK, the Dominican Sisters at Rögle Monastery in Sweden, and the South Australian Council of Churches.

oped out of the engagement of the Workgroup for Mission Theology at the Christian Council of Sweden and the Swedish Mission Council. The Workgroup focuses particularly on the role of mission in the churches, the academy, and in society. Receptive ecumenism supplied the means to support a process of learning about different ways of living and understanding mission. The Pilgrimage to the four different meeting places involved learning about mission in each of the four church families. At each meeting point of the journey, new knowledge was gained from the church family that hosted the place.

While receptive ecumenism might imply receiving knowledge from different kinds of sources, lecturers were a central source of knowledge during the Pilgrimage. All the lecturers who visited the four meeting places of the Pilgrimage were experienced and knowledgeable about the theme of mission in the life of their own church family. However, the lecturers did more than convey new knowledge; many of them also encouraged a self-critical way of learning. Each of them had been informed about the fundaments of receptive ecumenism. Therefore, it was not just the 'best china tea service' that was brought out through the lectures.[7] Difficulties and challenges in their churches' ways of living, managing, and thinking about mission were highlighted as well. This openness paved the way for frank and forthright conversation among the participants. The lecturers' gesture of 'reaching out their wounded hands' evoked echoes in the group.[8] Complex issues, such as proselytism and competition, formed a natural part of the participants' conversations from the very beginning of the Pilgrimage. As a method, receptive ecumenism helped people lower their guard and share self-critical reflection with other participants. It nurtured a safe environment for trustful and constructive dialogue on the multi-layered and contentious theme of mission.

The methodological starting points of receptive ecumenism, the format of the Pilgrimage, and the theme of mission all contributed significantly and gave stability to the development of the pedagogical process. They led to a process moreover which called for continuous monitoring of its variables such as the nature of the meeting places

---

7. The metaphor of 'the ecumenism of the best china tea service' is explicated in: Paul Murray 'Introducing Receptive Ecumenism' in *The Ecumenist. A Journal of Theology, Culture, and Society* 51/2 (2014): 4–5.

8. Murray's 'Introducing Receptive Ecumenism' also gives an account of receptive ecumenism as 'an ecumenism of the wounded hands' (see page 5).

and the internal dynamics of the group. However, an issue that also required special consideration was how to build a structure for such a pedagogical process. This part of the process will now be discussed and elucidated by using examples from the Pilgrimage.

Structure

Three Metaphors

Three metaphors from the Pilgrimage guided the way the structure of the pedagogical process was set up. The metaphors of *stillness, crossroads*, and *mountain* framed the pedagogical praxis of every meeting along the journey. These metaphors marked out the structure in the following ways.

The *stillness* gave opportunity for individual reflection on the principal question of receptive ecumenism; *'What is it that I and my tradition need to learn and receive, with integrity, from others?'*

The *crossroads* provided space for interactive meetings in small groups. In following up the individual reflections, participants from the same tradition considered the question *'What is it that we and our tradition need to learn and receive, with integrity, from others?'* Moreover, the *crossroads* provided a forum for talking over the same question in groups that gathered participants from different traditions.

The *mountain* was the meeting point of the whole group, with all its participants. Here, the group could sum up their discussions and discern overarching motifs which had guided the meeting. It gave the possibility to share individual reflections as well as insights resulting from the conversations of the small groups. The gatherings on the mountain framed the meeting, and also enabled stretching one's view out towards everyday life beyond the Pilgrimage.

The Pilgrimage involved a continuous development of the pedagogical process. The three metaphors provided significant starting points for this development. The structure, based in the metaphors of *stillness, crossroads*, and *mountain*, inspired different kinds of activities at every meeting. This structure formed an essential foundation for the modelling of different kinds of reflection and conversation practices. The activities, which were planned with due consideration given to the internal dynamics of the group and the nature of the meeting places, became increasingly adventurous as the pedagogical process proceeded. The study guide *Healing Gifts for Wounded Hands*, composed by the South Australian Council of Churches, was an important source of inspiration as the pedagogical process of the Pilgrimage was gradually developing.[9] In the following, this development is illustrated by examples from each of the four meeting places of the journey.

Examples

The First Meeting—Introducing the Structure

At the first meeting of the Pilgrimage, the participants of the group became acquainted with the structure of the pedagogical process. The structure of the *stillness*, the *crossroads*, and the *mountain* was introduced to them in a lecture, which also surveyed the foundations of receptive ecumenism.[10] The pedagogical structure of the first meeting formed a lasting pattern for the rest of the Pilgrimage. The *stillness* provided time and space for individual reflection on the lectures on mission. The group conversations at the *crossroads* followed on from the individual reflection. The *mountain* formed a meeting point for the whole group to interact, throughout the course of the meeting and at its conclusion. Every conclusion furthermore included a moment of stillness, which gave time for writing down one's reflections on the meeting.

The Second Meeting—Word and Image

The second meeting involved formulating as well as visualising one's learning on the theme of mission. At this meeting, verses and illustra-

---

9. South Australian Council of Churches (2014), *Healing Gifts for Wounded Hands. The Promise and Potential of Receptive Ecumenism*, <http://www.sacc.asn.au/_data/Healing_Gifts_for_Wounded_Hands_May_2014.pdf>. Accessed 6 May 2018.

10. The metaphors of *stillness, crossroads*, and *mountain* were introduced in the pedagogical process by Sven-Erik Fjellström. The introductory lecture was given by Sara Gehlin at St Ignatios Andliga Akademi, April 2017. This lecture presented the foundations of receptive ecumenism, while also connecting the three pilgrimage metaphors with the principles of receptive ecumenism as well as with the pedagogical practices presented in the study guide *Healing Gifts for Wounded Hands* (see note 9).

tions of Biblical narratives formed the point of departure for the participants' individual reflections in *stillness*. Here, one's understanding of mission was focused. These individual reflections fed into the meetings at the *crossroads*, where the conversations concentrated on the multiple understandings of mission that exist within each church family. On the *mountain*, the participants eventually illustrated, in words and images, the wide landscape of understandings which had come to light in the conversations at the crossroads. Thus, the theme of mission was brought to the fore in its breadth and depth. The work on Biblical narratives, which was introduced at the second meeting, was an essential feature of the remaining course of the Pilgrimage.

The Third Meeting—Fellow Pilgrims

'Curiosity' was the *leitmotif* of the third meeting of the Pilgrimage. The conversation model of the 'curiosity box', presented by the South Australian Council of Churches, inspired the preparation of this meeting.[11]

At this meeting, the *stillness*, which followed upon every lecture on mission, involved writing down one's questions about the content of the lectures. The questions, written on small pieces of paper, were then distributed in a number of 'curiosity boxes'. The curiosity boxes were eventually to become signposts for the approaching pilgrimage, where each participant would walk together with someone from another church family. Here, the *crossroads* implied being fellow pilgrims, who together followed a map through forests and over shores and meadows. The walk provided a forum for discussion on the questions that the participants had previously formulated. Along the path, a 'curiosity box' frequently turned up, full of new questions to talk over. The pilgrimage eventually involved new moments of *stillness*: first in meditation on a Bible verse that had been placed in the last 'curiosity box', and then in the chapel which was the geographical, physical goal of the pilgrimage on that occasion. The stillness in the chapel gave time for reflection on the conversations of the pilgrimage, with a special view to the question 'What is it that I and my tradition need to learn and receive, with integrity, from others?' The same

---

11. South Australian Council of Churches, *Healing Gifts for Wounded Hands*, 4–5.

question formed the starting point for the subsequent conversations at the *crossroads* with participants from their own church families.

The interaction on the *mountain* took place with the participants' questions in view. The questions from the 'curiosity boxes' were now collected in a circle on the floor. In this way, the concluding discussion evolved from the abundance of questions that the participants had formulated and from the way the theme of mission was experienced in the life and thought of the host-church family.

The Fourth Meeting—At Sea and by the Shore

A new dimension was added to the pedagogical process when the group gathered for the fourth and last time: the *water*. At this meeting, all pedagogical activities of reflection and conversation were located at the seashore or on the sea itself. Here, the *stillness*, which followed the lectures on mission, took place by the water. The shore was the place for individual reflection on the principal question of receptive ecumenism. The shore was also the place for the *crossroads*, where each participant could follow up their individual reflections together with someone from their own church family.

The *crossroads* also included accompanying a fellow participant from the host-church family. This time the conversations were carried out while canoeing. The time together at sea gave participants space for reflection on different ways of living and understanding mission within the host-church family. A few verses from the Bible supported the conversations. Since the meeting was the fourth and last one, the journey at sea formed a special occasion for sharing new perspectives which had emerged from the Pilgrimage as a whole. To journey by canoe was a voluntary activity and some participants choose to walk along the shore together.

The gathering on the *mountain* took place in two stages. To begin with, participants had the opportunity to share insights and perspectives from their conversations at sea and by the shore. Experiences and thoughts from the Pilgrimage were linked together. Finally, the group gathered at the bridge by the sea to participate in the concluding worship of the Pilgrimage.

Dynamics

As mentioned above, the Pilgrimage exemplified the way receptive ecumenism can nurture a trustful dialogue, where people are safe to lower their guard and open up to self-critical reflection. By means of its special focus on receiving and self-critical learning, receptive ecumenism reduced the fear of being questioned or subjected to someone else's agenda. In this way, receptive ecumenism stimulated the growth of mutual confidence among the participants.

At the same time, the Pilgrimage raised awareness of the importance of continuously considering the development of mutuality and confidence in the group. The fact that the pedagogical structure of the Pilgrimage could make space for an increasing adventurousness had its background in the mutual confidence that gradually developed among the participants. Their trust in each other allowed for pedagogical activities, which ranged from the conversation table to the reflections shared on the walking path and at sea. However, since different styles of conversation assume different levels of confidence, the pedagogical work involved considering each pedagogical activity in the light of the internal dynamics of the group.

Challenges

To lead a pedagogical process inspired by receptive ecumenism might involve dealing with certain challenges. On a number of occasions during the Pilgrimage, the very foundations of receptive ecumenism were questioned. Some limitations of the method were brought to light. When participants asked for critical viewpoints from their ecumenical fellows, receptive ecumenism with its exclusive focus on learning and receiving appeared insufficient. Since receptive ecumenism did not provide a forum for the critical debate that was called for, the question was asked whether receptive ecumenism runs the risk of fostering discussions that smooth over rather than manage ongoing conflicts.

The Pilgrimage moreover made apparent how the management of a pedagogical process based on receptive ecumenism might at times imply a balancing act. Those occasions when participants chose to scrutinise and level criticism at each other required sensitivity and care. A certain degree of diplomacy was needed to steer the conversation back to the starting point of learning and receiving, while not inhibiting the vitality of the conversation or the creativity of the group.

Timeframes

The Pilgrimage gave good reason to consider closely the question of timeframes. Other initiatives have demonstrated that pedagogical processes grounded in receptive ecumenism can be carried out within a variety of timeframes. There are projects that have comprised a series of meetings within predetermined limits. In other cases, learning processes have been launched without setting any end date. Some projects have comprised only two gatherings with homework between the meetings; yet other projects have only had one single gathering. Receptive ecumenism has also shaped longstanding collaborations of several years' duration.[12]

During the Pilgrimage, the pedagogical process was supported by a generous timeframe, which spanned a period of almost two years where an afternoon, evening, and morning could be set aside for each of the four meetings. The Pilgrimage gave insight into the way receptive ecumenism involves the gradual formation of attitudes and new viewpoints, and therefore entails a slow process. The pedagogical process was similarly served by the long-term planning that was possible, and this supported the stability of the group and enhanced the continuity of meetings. While timeframes are an essential factor in the construction of pedagogical projects, a related question concerns the goals that this work aims to achieve within those parameters.

Goals

The Pilgrimage was carried out in full awareness of the variety of goals a pedagogical process inspired by receptive ecumenism might aim to fulfil. The renewal of ecclesiological structures is one goal, which frequently appears in literature on receptive ecumenism. Another is the goal of achieving a deeper understanding of one's own and others' theological traditions—a vital part of receptive ecumenical striving

---

12. The examples derive from the ecumenical work that is carried out at the initiative of the South Australian Council of Churches and the Centre for Catholic Studies at Durham University in the UK, as well as by the Anglican Roman Catholic International Commission and Jönköping Christian Co-operation Council in Sweden.

towards interior church reform.[13] Receptive ecumenical processes have proved that the methodological agenda underlying the strivings towards these goals can also generate other results that are well worth considering. By means of its focus on self-critical learning from the other, receptive ecumenism can result in the building of trust and the reduction of fear in ecumenical encounters. The construction of attitudes grounded in trust and an in-depth understanding of the other can become a goal in itself.[14]

Against this background, it can be concluded that receptive ecumenism can lead to several results at the same time. This was exemplified during the Pilgrimage, which fulfilled its overarching goal. The participants gained a deeper knowledge of the ways in which mission is lived and understood within the four church families. The Pilgrimage resulted in mutual enrichment between traditions. On the way, however, receptive ecumenism generated results that reached beyond the sphere of thought. While searching for increased knowledge and understanding, interpersonal trust and ecumenical friendship were strengthened. The journey to the four places, with the goal of receiving a deeper knowledge of each other's traditions, also resulted in the experience of receiving a deeper confidence and trust in the other.

Bibliography

Gehlin, Sara, 'Receptiv ekumenik – en pedagogisk process', Forthcoming.

Gehlin, Sara, 'Receptiv ekumenik – om hopp och tillit i ekumeniska relationer', in *Var inte rädd – en bok om hopp* edited by Dag Tuvelius (Förbundet Kristen Humanism, 2017), 89–98.

---

13. See for example Antonia Pizzey, 'On the Maturation of Receptive Ecumenism. The Connection between Receptive Ecumenism and Spiritual Ecumenism' in *Pacifica: Australasian Theological Studies,* 28/2 (2015): 110–18; Ormond Rush, 'Receptive Ecumenism and Discerning the *Sensus Fidelium.* Expanding the Categories for a Catholic Reception of Revelation', in *Theological Studies,* 70/3 (2017): 559–72; Sara Gehlin, 'Receptiv ekumenik – *om hopp och tillit i ekumeniska relationer' in Var inte rädd – en bok om hopp',* edited by Dag Tuvelius (Förbundet Kristen Humanism, 2017), 89–98. See also the anthology *Receptive Ecumenism and the Call to Catholic Learning. Exploring a Way for Contemporary Ecumenism* edited by Paul D Murray (Oxford University Press, 2008).

14. See also Mary-Anne Plaatjies van Huffel, 'From Conciliar Ecumenism to Transformative Receptive Ecumenism', in *HTS Teologiese Studies/Theological Studies,* 73/3 (2017): 6–8.

Murray, Paul D, 'Introducing Receptive Ecumenism', in *The Ecumenist. A Journal of Theology, Culture, and Society,* 51/2 (2014): 1–7.

Murray, Paul D, editor, *Receptive Ecumenism and the Call to Catholic Learning. Exploring a Way for Contemporary Ecumenism* (Oxford University Press, 2008).

Pizzey, Antonia, 'On the Maturation of Receptive Ecumenism. The Connection between Receptive Ecumenism and Spiritual Ecumenism', in *Pacifica: Australasian Theological Studies,* 28/2 (2015): 108–25.

Plaatjies van Huffel, Mary-Anne, 'From Conciliar Ecumenism to Transformative Receptive Ecumenism', in *HTS Teologiese Studies/ Theological Studies,* 73/3 (2017): 1–13.

Rush, Ormond, 'Receptive Ecumenism and Discerning the *Sensus Fidelium.* Expanding the Categories for a Catholic Reception of Revelation', in *Theological Studies.* 70/3 (2017): 559–72

South Australian Council of Churches, *Healing Gifts for Wounded Hands. The Promise and Potential of Receptive Ecumenism,* <http:// www.sacc.asn.au/_data/Healing_Gifts_for_Wounded_Hands_ May_2014.pdf>. Accessed 3 April 2018.

'Receiving Women's Gifts': An Exploration of the Role of Hospitality in the Practice of Receptive Ecumenism

Gabrielle R Thomas

Introduction[1]

At the Fourth International Conference on Receptive Ecumenism in Canberra, November 2017, Antonia Pizzey identified hospitality as one of the 'core values' or 'virtues' required for the flourishing of Receptive Ecumenism.[2] To explore what this might look like in practice, I shall discuss a case-study which focuses upon the ecumenical work of a small group of Christian women, who, inspired by this way of engaging ecumenically, have organised and hosted small-scale Receptive Ecumenism gatherings in England; the aim of these gatherings is to create a space for women, who come from varied Christian traditions, to learn and receive gifts from one another. Through reflecting theologically upon their practices, important learning arises, which, I argue, informs the particular nature of hospitality necessary for the flourishing of Receptive Ecumenism. Further to this, through reflecting upon the women's practices against the backdrop of Christ's radical hospitality, a prophetic call unfolds, which challenges the churches' own hospitality to women and their reception of women's gifts.

---

1. An extended version of this essay will be published in Brill's ecumenical journal, *Exchange,* under the title 'A Call for Hospitality: Learning from a Particular Example of Women's Grass Roots Practice of Receptive Ecumenism in the UK' (forthcoming, November 2018).
2. Antonia Pizzey, 'The Receptive Ecumenical Spirit: the Role of the Virtues in Guiding Receptive Ecumenical Discernment and Decision-Making', *Fourth International Conference on Receptive Ecumenism: Discernment, Decision Making and Reception* in Canberra, Australia, November 2017; <http://arts-ed.csu.edu.au/__data/assets/pdf_file/0005/2875415/Leaning-into-the-Spirit-Conference-booklet.pdf>. Accessed 30 January 2018. I am indebted to Antonia Pizzey and Sara Gehlin, who generously shared their unpublished work with me.

I begin by outlining briefly Receptive Ecumenism, as it is understood and practised by the particular women in question, before
moving on to introduce the women themselves. One metaphor, by
way of a description, which the women favour, is a tea party. In England, 'High Tea' is a tradition in which the host or hostess brings out
all their best china and puts it on the table for the guests, covered
with delicious food. On these occasions, the convention is to use the
best china and crockery that one has in one's home. Sometimes, when
churches come together ecumenically, it can be a little like an English
'High Tea', in which the churches share only the best of themselves.
As the women understand it, 'Receptive Ecumenism turns this idea
upside down'.[3] When diverse churches meet to engage in Receptive Ecumenism, the idea is that they do not use their best 'china' or
crockery. Instead, they come to the table, bringing with them all the
broken, chipped and old pieces of crockery which they own. With
their broken plates on the table, they ask another church whether
that church has anything in her tradition which would help mend the
chipped plates?

Receptive Ecumenism creates space for churches to pause, examine themselves and ask, 'where are we broken?' or, 'are there areas
of church life which need healing?'[4] Having identified an area which
requires healing, a church seeks to learn from another tradition
regarding respective practices. Thus, one church asks of another,
'what gifts might you share which help towards healing the areas in
which we are wounded?' A church holds out her hands to receive the
gifts from another tradition; a key feature of the open hands is that
they bear wounds which need healing, rather than being hands which
are already whole. After key learnings have been shared, a church
moves on to discern which gifts it may receive with integrity.

Case Study

Whilst ecumenists have discussed hospitality conceptually, as far
as I am aware, the outworking of hospitality within Receptive Ecu-

---

3. I apply quotation marks when I cite the women directly.
4. Paul D Murray, 'Searching the Living Truth of the Church in Practice: On the
   Transformative Task of Systematic Ecclesiology', in *Modern Theology* 29/4 (2013):
   251–81.

menism at grass roots has not yet been explored.[5] During 2017–18, I have been journeying with members of the Ecumenical and Interfaith Group of the National Board of Catholic Women in the United Kingdom, engaging with them through participant observation, formal one-to-one interviews and informal conversations. The hospitality I (as an Anglican priest and researcher) received from these women, during individual and group interviews, spending time with them informally, and through participating in their conferences, inspired me to explore the role of hospitality in Receptive Ecumenism. In various forms, the women have worked together ecumenically across a number of church traditions for over thirty years. Since 2013, they have organised and hosted gatherings in order that women may engage with one another through practising Receptive Ecumenism. Just over one hundred women have participated to date, from churches as diverse as Assemblies of God, Salvation Army, Anglican, Catholic, Orthodox, Methodist, Baptist and United Reformed. The roles the women attending have played within their churches vary from ordained, holy orders, through to women who serve in children's ministries or organise refreshments. Below is an outline of a typical conference:

- Welcome with Tea/Coffee/Snacks
- Prayer and Scripture Reflection
- Introduction to Receptive Ecumenism
- Four Short Talks by women from different traditions
- Gathering together for discussion in small groups
- Lunch
- Group discussions based around the theme and talks; the practising of Receptive Ecumenism
- Gathering together the themes and feedback
- Closing Prayer and Farewell.

---

5. This reflection is situated within broader research conducted in conjunction with the Ecumenical and Interfaith Group of the National Board of Catholic Women, with whom I am working to explore the experiences of women who work in English churches through Receptive Ecumenism. All data gathered is recorded, transcribed, analysed and used only with permission. 'The National Board of Catholic Women actively seeks to promote the presence, participation and responsibilities of Catholic Women in the Church and society, in order to enable them to fulfil their evangelical mission and to work for the common good'; <http://www.nbcw.co.uk>. Accessed 22 March 2018.

Since I regularly meet Christians who have not heard of Receptive Ecumenism, I was curious to learn what it was about this way of ecumenical engagement that had inspired the women to the extent that they should want to put it into action. They explained that they had initially heard about it through their connections with the Centre for Catholic Studies at Durham University, UK. The women had been drawn initially to the emphasis on 'listening, learning and receiving gifts' from other Christian traditions. Added to this, each of the women believes 'churches should be in unity.' They spoke to me about how they believed 'the Holy Spirit has inspired and guided' their work. Seeing 'new possibilities for ecumenism through the fresh approach offered by Receptive Ecumenism' and as another woman commented, 'it is an interesting aspect of ecumenism which is worth exploring', they decided to 'put it to the test'.

From enveloping the day in prayer and Scripture reflection through to refreshments and lunch, the women's beliefs about and practices of hospitality underline the organisation and duration of the gatherings. The women's practices develop our understanding of the practice of hospitality within Receptive Ecumenism, highlighting key points to consider. When considered in light of Christ's own radical hospitality, I argue that the women's practice serves as a prophetic call to the churches regarding their own hospitality to women and reception of women's gifts.

Hospitality at the Receptive Ecumenism Gatherings

Scripture and the Christian tradition witness to God's hospitality.[6] This is recognised in the uniqueness of the incarnation of Christ in which God demonstrates radically God's hospitality to the whole world, through to the simple breaking of bread shared on the road to Emmaus, in which Jesus is revealed as both host and guest (Lk 24:13–35). As we turn to the specific practices of hospitality within the Receptive Ecumenism gathering facilitated by the group of women in question, we will move through the way the gathering is organised.

---

6. For example; David B Gowler, *Host, Guest, Enemy, and Friend: Portraits of the Pharisees in Luke and Acts* (New York: Peter Lang, 1991); Luke Bretherton, *Hospitality as Holiness: Christian Witness Amid Moral Diversity* (New York: Routledge, 2006).

We will observe a kind of hospitality which not only welcomes and learns from the stranger, but also creates a safe space for gifts to be received. Moreover, I argue, the hospitality offered points to important learning for the practice of Receptive Ecumenism.

The question of where to host the gatherings was an important consideration to the group. They wanted to use well their position of power as hosts; one of the group observed that it was 'important not to hold the gathering on Catholic ground'. Another woman commented, 'we wanted to create a space in which we were received as well as receiving so that it is truly receptive'. Thus, they opted to host the conference in a village hall, sharing the hosting with others. By making this move, they were both received and receiving.

As the women gather together from various parts of England, tea/coffee and biscuits/cake are offered. The food and drink on arrival 'provides refreshment for those who have travelled to the gathering, at the same time providing space for women to gather themselves for the day ahead'. The English custom of drinking tea is often equated with being made to feel at ease; this, in turn sets the scene for a comfortable space in which guests may begin to feel safe. Safety of the participants is crucial to Receptive Ecumenism, as we shall discuss shortly.

Once the women are refreshed, the day begins in prayer and a reflection on Scripture. The group's rationale behind this is that 'hospitality begins in God, expressing an aspect of God's character'. Through beginning in prayer, we locate ourselves and our stories in God. As one of the women commented, 'prayer together affirms that it is the Spirit who we trust to lead us forward into unity'. Through prayer, both the hosts and guests are locating God as the host, who provides for their needs.

Following prayer, Scripture reflection and a brief introduction to Receptive Ecumenism, 'four women from different Christian traditions speak about their experience of living in their tradition'. Women from various churches speak on a particular topic which has been agreed upon beforehand. For example, women from Baptist, Catholic, Anglican and Assemblies of God churches might speak on their views, experience and practice of various forms of ministry. The women I spoke to were keen to emphasise that they 'discussed ministry with a small 'm', since Catholic women are not permitted to enter into ordained ministry'.[7] These talks allow the women present to enter into each other's worlds, at least with respect to their churches, and there is an opportunity to explore the differences in each other's church. Through listening to one another, the women are able 'to discern more clearly through prayer and discussion the wounds and gifts of their own traditions'. One of the group spoke about how 'we thought long and hard about the topics, because we wanted to address issues which are relevant to women . . . we've seen a lot of men in press photographs concerned with Receptive Ecumenism and we wanted to create space for women to receive from one another'.[8]

Following these talks, the women present are invited to gather into smaller groups to begin to reflect on what they have heard in relation to their own context and church tradition. After lunch, these groups continue; through careful facilitation, the women discuss challenges and reflect upon gifts which might be received.

The fact that these small groups consist of only women raises an important question regarding to whom hospitality is offered at these conferences. During our time together, I witnessed the women discussing at length the issue of whether groups should be mixed or women-only. As one woman commented, 'the decision to restrict the gathering to women-only was not made lightly'. Since research demonstrates that women are more inclined to speak in groups in which women only are present, the organisers decided 'to restrict the gatherings to women so that women would be able to speak as freely as possible'.[9] Further to this, one of the group said, 'women needed to be given the opportunity to speak uninterrupted and not be diminished'. It was her belief that a mixed group would not provide such a 'free space for women to share safely'. Power and safety are key issues within Receptive Ecumenism. Feeling safe is essential, since exposing

---

7. John Paul II spoke on containing the tradition of reserving priestly ordination to men alone in the Roman Catholic Church in his Apostolic Letter, 'Ordinatio Sacerdotalis', <https://w2.vatican.va/content/john-paul-ii/en/apost_letters/1994/documents/hf_jp-ii_apl_19940522_ordinatio-sacerdotalis.html>. Accessed 10 May 2018.

8. One such example is the third phase of ARCIC in which 4 of the 22 participants are women; <https://www.anglicancentreinrome.org/Groups/194769/Anglican_Centre_in/What_we_do/Ecumenical_Dialogues/ARCIC_III/ARCIC_III.aspx>. Accessed 31 May 2018.

9. Gloria Bonder, *The New Information Technologies and Women: Essential Reflections* (Santiago, Chile: United Nations Publications, 2003), 30.

wounds renders a person and/or a Church vulnerable; therefore this move is made more successfully if the one bearing wounds experiences a safe environment.

This relates to broader issues, which arise in light of asymmetrical relations. For example, an ordained Anglican woman commented, 'I am not sure I would want to come vulnerably with wounded hands into a space where my ministry is not recognised'.[10] Whilst she was not speaking on behalf of all women, she raises a serious question with which we must grapple in relation to hospitality within Receptive Ecumenism. We must contend for the best practice which creates the space for women to be involved in all levels of Receptive Ecumenism, from grass roots through to formal discussions, recognising that women 'can make a valuable contribution'. Believing that 'God affirms all women', the women have created a space in which women may freely and as safely as possible share their gifts.

I argue that the women's practice, of both listening to and receiving one another's ministries, embodies the kind of radical hospitality practised by Christ in the New Testament. To make sense of my claim, we turn to the themes of purity and holiness which run through Old and New Testaments.

Hospitality, Purity and Holiness

In his book *Hospitality as Holiness*, Luke Bretherton writes, 'Through his hospitality, which has as its focal point actual feasting and table fellowship, Jesus turns the world upside down'.[11] In the New Testament, Jesus brings together holiness and hospitality in a particular way 'by inverting their relations: hospitality becomes the means of holiness'.[12] For example, in Luke-Acts, the Pharisees only eat food with the people with whom they share the same values.[13] Therefore, their strict purity regulations mean that there are restrictions on their hospital-

---

10. It is worth noting that whilst the Catholic Church formally and as an institution does not currently accept the validity of women's ordination, many of the members of the Catholic Church do recognise the validity of women's ordination.
11. Bretherton, *Hospitality as Holiness*, 129.
12. Bretherton, *Hospitality as Holiness*, 129.
13. Jerome H Neyrey, 'The Social Word of Luke-Acts', in *The Social World of Luke-Acts*, edited by Jerome H Neyrey (Peabody, Massachusetts: Hendrickson Publishers, 1992), 361–88, at page 364.

ity. For the Pharisees, true holiness means limited hospitality. They 'criticise Jesus . . . for eating with tax collectors and sinners, because shared table fellowship implies that Jesus shares *their* world not God's world of holiness'.[14] In other words, Christ's hospitality of gentiles, sinners and those who are elsewhere considered 'tainted' or 'impure', demonstrates his holiness because he restores them rather than being contaminated by them and thus requiring cleansing himself.

Let us consider how this works out in action by examining Luke 8:43–48, which describes the encounter between Jesus and a woman who has been bleeding for many years: 'She came up behind him and touched the fringe of his clothes, and immediately her haemorrhage stopped' (v 44). Following usual purity laws, Jesus would have gone to the temple to be cleansed after experiencing physical contact from a bleeding woman, since she would be considered unclean. However, rather than requiring cleansing, Jesus' holiness contagiously cleanses the woman. He heals her, restoring her to a right place amongst her people, rather than she tainting him. Later in Luke 10, Jesus tells the well-known parable of the Samaritan man, which recalls the demonstration of hospitality by a man who would be considered unclean by the Pharisees. Rather than using the parable to endorse purity teachings, Jesus tells those listening to 'Go and do likewise' (v 10:37) that is, to go and show mercy to those outside the confines of their social and religious world. Thus, through actions and parables Jesus establishes a way of being, in which mercy and hospitality to those who are 'unclean' is prized. Noteworthy is that not only is this approach to holiness and hospitality inhabited by Jesus, but Christ establishes this as the preferred behaviour of his followers. This is mapped on to Acts 10, when Peter visits Cornelius, a Roman centurion and declares 'You yourselves know that it is unlawful for a Jew to associate with or to visit a Gentile; but God has shown me that I should not call anyone profane or unclean' (10:28). Later in the chapter (v 10:44) the Holy Spirit falls upon the Gentiles present, thus affirming Peter's inclusion of them.

Conclusion

In light of this, let us recall the women gathering to engage in Receptive Ecumenism and turn to reflect upon the hospitality offered to

---

14. Neyrey, 'The Social Word of Luke-Acts', 364.

each woman present. Whilst many women flourish in churches and are fulfilled in various vocations, this is not true for all women. There is not space enough to cite the vast body of literature which calls for a reception of each woman's gifts in the Body of Christ.[15] Even today, women's gifts are frequently rejected, especially if the gifts relate to teaching and preaching, or leadership. Added to this, many women have testified that little hospitality is offered regarding their involvement in the processes of decision-making and leadership of churches.[16] Through Receptive Ecumenism, after listening to one another, there is space for the women gathered to receive one another's gifts, even if these gifts are being rejected within the structural level of some of the churches. For example, women who testify to a vocation to preach, but are not allowed to pursue this in their own church, are provided with a space not only to be affirmed, but also received as preachers.

Thus, in the same way that Jesus radically redefines hospitality by receiving and affirming those who are previously impure in relation to Torah, these gatherings of women function as a safe space where gifts are received which are otherwise rejected by churches.

Reflecting upon the practice of hospitality within the small-scale Receptive Ecumenism conferences highlights important learning for Receptive Ecumenism more broadly. First, these gatherings emphasise the importance of prayer, with regards to recognising that hospitality begins in God, and all gifts come from God. Also, it serves as a reminder that we look to the Spirit to lead the churches into transformation. Secondly, the conferences raise questions pertaining to power: How do we use our power as hosts? Which location should we choose for Receptive Ecumenism? If the discussion is on a formal level: Whom do we invite? Who is excluded? Where rela-

---

15. See for example, Elisabeth Behr-Sigel, *The Ministry of Women in the Church*, translated by Stephen Bigham (Pasadena, California: Oakwood Publications, 1991); Rosemary Radford Ruether, 'Imago Dei, Christian Tradition and Feminist Hermeneutics', in *Image of God and Gender Models in Judaeo-Christian Tradition*, edited by Kari Elisabeth Børresen (Oslo: Solum Forag, 1991), 258–81; Eileen R Campbell-Reed, 'Living Testaments: How Catholic and Baptist Women in Ministry Both Judge and Renew the Church', in *Ecclesial Practices*, 4/2 (2017): 167–98.

16. <https://www.futurechurch.org/women-in-church-leadership/women-in-church-leadership/action/tips-for-advancing-women-in-church>. Accessed 15 March 2018.

tions are asymmetrical: What can we do to ensure this is attended to with integrity? Thirdly, the conferences determine the importance of safety, especially when asking individuals or churches to expose wounds. This can be expressed broadly, reaching from refreshments throughout a gathering, listening to and learning from the stranger, through to the more careful consideration of who is present. Whilst Receptive Ecumenism speaks of churches learning from one another, these conferences highlight that churches consist of persons, and each individual person present must feel safe for the flourishing of Receptive Ecumenism.

Lastly, when considered in light of Christ's own radical hospitality which receives and restores the stranger, I argue, the women's gathering for Receptive Ecumenism at grass roots serves as a prophetic voice, which not only calls to account the hospitality of our churches to women, but also calls for the reception of the whole breadth of women's gifts across the churches.

Bibliography

ARCIC III <https://www.anglicancentreinrome.org/Groups/194769/Anglican_Centre_in/What_we_do/Ecumenical_Dialogues/ARCIC_III/ARCIC_III.aspx>. Accessed 6 May 2018.

Behr-Sigel, Elisabeth, *The Ministry of Women in the Church*, translated by Stephen Bigham (Pasadena, California: Oakwood Publications, 1991).

Bonder, Gloria, *The New Information Technologies and Women: Essential Reflections* (Santiago, Chile: United Nations Publications, 2003).

Bretherton, Luke, *Hospitality as Holiness: Christian Witness Amid Moral Diversity* (New York: Routledge, 2006).

Campbell-Reed, Eileen R, 'Living Testaments: How Catholic and Baptist Women in Ministry Both Judge and Renew the Church', in *Ecclesial Practices* 4/2 (2017): 167–98.

Fourth International Conference on Receptive Ecumenism: Discernment, Decision Making and Reception in Canberra, Australia, November 2017, <http://arts-ed.csu.edu.au/__data/assets/pdf_file/0005/2875415/Leaning-into-the-Spirit-Conference-booklet.pdf>. Accessed 6 May 2018.

Future Church website, <https://futurechurch.org>. Accessed 6 May 2018.

Gowler, David, *Host, Guest, Enemy, and Friend: Portraits of the Pharisees in Luke and Acts* (New York: Peter Lang, 1991).

Murray, Paul D, 'Searching the Living Truth of the Church in Practice: On the Transformative Task of Systematic Ecclesiology', in *Modern Theology*, 29/4 (2013): 251–81.

National Board of Catholic Women website, <http://www.nbcw.co.uk>. Accessed 6 May 2018.

Neyrey, Jerome H, 'The Social Word of Luke-Acts', in *The Social World of Luke-Acts*, edited by Jerome H Neyrey (Peabody, Massachusetts: Hendrickson Publishers, 1992), 361–88.

'Ordinatio Sacerdotalis', <https://w2.vatican.va/content/john-paul-ii/en/apost_letters/1994/documents/hf_jp-ii_apl_19940522_ordinatio-sacerdotalis.html>. Accessed 6 May 2018.

Radford Ruether, Rosemary, 'Imago Dei, Christian Tradition and Feminist Hermeneutics', in *Image of God and Gender Models in Judaeo-Christian Tradition*, edited by Kari Elisabeth Børresen (Oslo: Solum Forag, 1991), 258–81.

'Receiving with Dynamic Integrity': Ecumenical Commitments and Reception Hermeneutics

Gregory A Ryan

Introduction

'Are we receiving Receptive Ecumenism?' So asked the Anglican ecclesiologist Paul Avis in an incisive 2012 essay which unpacks some of the key proposals made by Paul Murray and others, and sets them in relationship to established ecumenical dialogues and challenges.[1] If we were to attempt an answer today, we might look at the evidence of how these principles have been applied in a range of ecclesial contexts, and evaluate the potential for further fruitful applications. To name just three of the most significant examples, such an approach could consider the following: the adoption of Receptive Ecumenism as the methodology for the third phase of Anglican-Roman Catholic International Commission (ARCIC);[2] the publication of resources for local churches in England and Australia based on this approach;[3] and the address given by Archbishop Justin Welby for the seventieth anniversary of the World Council of Churches in which he said that 'one

---

1. Paul Avis, 'Are We Receiving "Receptive Ecumenism"?', in *Ecclesiology*, 8/2 (2012): 223–34.
2. The use of Receptive Ecumenism in the current phase of ARCIC is noted in a number of communiques, the most recent being issued after the Seventh ARCIC III meeting, in Erfurt (14–20 May 2017): <www.anglicancommunion.org/relationships/ecumenical-dialogues/roman-catholic/arcic.aspx >. The fruits of this approach are expected to be seen in an agreed statement, *Walking Together on the Way: Learning to be Church—Local, Regional, Universal* (The 'Erfurt Document'), to be published in 2018.
3. For example, in Australia: South Australian Council of Churches, *Healing Gifts for Wounded Hands*, at <http://www.sacc.asn.au/_data/Healing_Gifts_for_Wounded_Hands_May_2014.pdf>; in England, Callan Slipper, *Enriched by the Other: A Spiritual Guide to Receptive Ecumenism*, (Cambridge: Grove, 2016).

of the most important of recent ecumenical developments has been the concept of "Receptive Ecumenism".[4]

However, this is not the only way of evaluating the approach. Adapting the title of an article by Paul and Andrea Murray, I suggest that not only the range and reach, but also the *roots* of Receptive Ecumenism require ongoing attention.[5] Indeed, it is precisely because of the apparent ease with which Receptive Ecumenism has been received that there is a need to consider the theological and hermeneutical roots of this distinctive approach, if it is to realise its potential as a distinctive ecumenical strategy. The simplicity and attractiveness of the basic principle—which is undoubtedly one of the strengths of Murray's approach—brings with it a concomitant risk of over-easy appropriations springing up in shallow ground. At the very least, the expanding range and reach of Receptive Ecumenism has given rise to some diverse and surprising interpretations. For example, it has recently been described as asking one's ecumenical partners 'what gifts from their tradition we might find useful . . . like showing a colleague an article one has written and saying "tell me what you make of my argumentation".[6] More widely, Receptive Ecumenism has been viewed in relationship to established ecumenical ideas, such as an exchange of gifts[7] or as a kind of Spiritual Ecumenism.[8] Cer-

---

4. Justin Welby, "'Ecumenical Spring": Archbishop Justin's speech at World Council of Churches 70th Anniversary', at <www.archbishopofcanterbury.org/speaking-and-writing/speeches/ecumenical-spring-archbishop-justins-speech-world-council-churches>. Accessed 10 April 2018.

5. Paul D Murray and Andrea L Murray, 'The Roots, Range and Reach of Receptive Ecumenism', in *Unity in Process*, edited by Clive Barrett (London: Darton Longman & Todd, 2012), 79–94. In the original article 'roots' refers to the personal life-narratives from which the project emerged, whilst 'range' addressed the theological scope. I am using roots as the metaphor for the undergirding theological framework, whilst range and reach refer to the potential and actualised fruitfulness of Receptive Ecumenism.

6. Tracey Rowlands, 'Ecumenism—What Future?', at '<www.catholicweekly.com.au/prof-tracey-rowlands-ordinariate-lecture-ecumenism-what-future/>. Accessed 10 April 2018.

7. See for example, Margaret O'Gara, 'Receiving Gifts in Ecumenical Dialogue', in *Receptive Ecumenism and the Call to Catholic Learning*, edited by Paul D Murray (Oxford and New York: Oxford University Press, 2008), 26–38.

8. Antonia Pizzey, 'On the Maturation of Receptive Ecumenism: The Connection between Receptive Ecumenism and Spiritual Ecumenism' in *Pacifica: Australasian Theological Studies*, 28/2 (2015): 108–25.

tainly Receptive Ecumenism has a close affinity with the notion of gift exchange found in *Ut Unum Sint* [9] but part of the distinctiveness of Murray's approach is its unilateral character, which does not wait on the other party receiving first. In this regard, it is closer to the attitude expressed by Pope Francis in 2017:

> Authentic reconciliation between Christians will only be achieved when we can acknowledge each other's gifts and learn from one another, with humility and docility, without waiting for the others to learn first.[10]

There can be no doubt that it also has deep roots—and perhaps untapped potential—in Spiritual Ecumenism, but it is also engaged with questions of theological method, interpretation and development of doctrine, as well as with analysing and renewing ecclesial structures and practice, and with the appropriation of hermeneutical and philosophical resources.

To a certain extent, a spectrum of diverse interpretations is to be expected. After all, Murray has made it clear that Receptive Ecumenism is not a brand, not a carefully managed franchise, but rather an 'ad-hoc strategy', a 'virtuous virus' at the heart of which is 'a total ethic as simple and all pervasive as the gospel it represents'.[11] In order to explore this ethic by attending to the roots of Receptive Ecumenism, I will first revisit the hinterland of Paul Murray's work on theological rationality from which Receptive Ecumenism emerges, and draw out some of the most significant methodological commitments. Secondly, I hope to show that these commitments resonate with a surprisingly little used resource in Receptive Ecumenism, namely reception hermeneutics, which I will approach through the work of Ormond Rush. The complementary approaches of Murray and Rush can be named respectively as 'dynamic integrity' and 'rejuvenating reception'.

---

9. Pope John Paul II, '*Ut Unum Sint*: Encyclical on Commitment to Ecumenism' (25 May 1995), at <w2.vatican.va/content/john-paul-ii/en/encyclicals/documents/hf_jp-ii_enc_25051995_ut-unum-sint.html>. Accessed 10 April 2018.

10. Pope Francis, 'Celebration of Vespers on the Solemnity of the Conversion of Saint Paul the Apostle' (25 January 2017) at < w2.vatican.va/content/francesco/en/homilies/2017/documents/papa-francesco_20170125_vespri-conversione-san-paolo.html>. Accessed 10 April 2018.

11. Paul D Murray, 'Receptive Ecumenism and Catholic Learning: Establishing the Agenda', in *Receptive Ecumenism and the Call to Catholic Learning*, edited by Paul D Murray (Oxford and New York: Oxford University Press, 2008), 5–25, at 16.

Dynamic Integrity

'Dynamic integrity' is a concept which can be found throughout Murray's writings, but which I am using here to describe his over-all methodological strategy, of which Receptive Ecumenism is one outworking.[12] The commitments which this involves are indicated in his programmatic essay at the start of *Receptive Ecumenism and the Call to Catholic Learning*.[13] Having identified the present ecumenical context as a site of postmodern concerns about 'traditioned particularity', Murray draws on the pragmatist tradition, especially the work of the philosopher Nicholas Rescher[14] in order to propose a mode of theological reflection which on the one hand does not rely on some neutral objective ground from which a position can be proved regardless of where one is standing, and on the other hand rejects what he describes as 'closed, relativistic tribalism'. The key thinking at work in Receptive Ecumenism, we are told, has been shaped in no small part through this engagement. The first question to answer, then, is: what is the nature of this shaping influence?

Firstly, against the kind of postmodern relativism advocated by Richard Rorty,[15] Murray follows Rescher in maintaining a concern for truth and a conviction that however elusive and difficult identify-

---

12. '"Dynamic integrity" is intended to articulate both the continuous identity and the contextually specific freshness that are each always authentic to Christian tradition... It is intended also to resonate with Francis Sullivan's evocative phrase 'creative fidelity' while suggesting a greater degree of expansive reconfiguration in the light of fresh data, experience, concerns, perspectives, methodologies, concepts and beliefs than Sullivan's own analysis suggests.' Paul D Murray, 'Discerning the Dynamics of Doctrinal Development: A Post-Foundationalist Perspective', in *Faithful Reading: New Essays in Theology in Honour of Fergus Kerr, OP*, edited by Simon Oliver, Karen Kilby, and Thomas O'Loughlin (London: T&T Clark, 2012), 193–220, at 215.

13. Murray, 'Establishing the Agenda'.

14. Nicholas Rescher, *A System of Pragmatic Idealism*, volume 1. *Human Knowledge in Idealistic Perspective*, (Princeton: Princeton University Press, 1992); volume 2, *The Validity of Values* (Princeton: Princeton University Press, 1993); volume 3, *Metaphilosophical Inquiries* (Princeton: Princeton University Press, 1994). For Murray's substantial engagement with Rescher see Paul D Murray, *Reason, Truth, and Theology in Pragmatist Perspective* (Leuven: Peeters, 2004), 91–130 and 133–61.

15. Richard Rorty, *Philosophy and the Mirror of Nature* (Princeton: Princeton University Press, 1979). For Murray's critique, see Murray, *Reason, Truth, and Theology*, 25–90.

ing truth may be, we are closer to it when we pursue it than when we abandon the quest. This is one reason why Receptive Ecumenism is not satisfied with an 'ecumenism of life' alone. Second, key values from Rescher are foregrounded and appropriated by Murray who argues that theological reasoning needs to be *recursive (or iterative)*, *expansive* and *self-critical (or fallibilist)*. These principles are explicitly cited in regard of Receptive Ecumenism.[16] Finally, Rescher's 'committed pluralism' is endorsed as 'uniquely well-suited to the contemporary Christian ecumenical context and to indicating a constructive way forwards.'[17] This position both acknowledges the pluralist reality of the world *and* the legitimacy of making a rational claim for holding one of those positions rather than another, through continually testing the coherence of that position against multiple criteria.

To understand the kind of coherence Murray envisages requires us to look wider than the introductory essays on Receptive Ecumenism and turn to his work on the development of doctrine.[18] The outline of what Murray has in mind can in fact be stated quite simply. A coherent system—for example of doctrine and practice in a particular tradition—must exhibit *internal coherence* (such as is found in intra-textual reading of scripture or interpreting doctrine as an organic whole). But if a tradition is also to be expansive—one of the characteristics inherited from Rescher—then an *extrinsic coherence* is also required as new horizons in the world and other traditions are encountered. Here we need to remember that part of the distinctiveness of Receptive Ecumenism is that it is orientated, at least initially, not to direct consensus *between* traditions but refreshing, expanding, healing *within* a tradition through learning from the other. Ecclesial learning, as Murray conceives it, is envisaged not as instrumental but as transformative.

The originality of Murray's contribution is seen most clearly in his addition of practical fruitfulness as a criterion of truth through the notion of *pragmatic coherence*, giving his coherentist approach three dimensions or criteria: internal coherence, extensive or extrinsic coherence, and pragmatic coherence. In an essay linking systematic and practical ecclesiology, Murray sets Receptive Ecumenism firmly

---

16. For a fuller account of these methodological commitments, see Murray, *Reason, Truth, and Theology*, 133–61.
17. Murray, 'Establishing the Agenda', 8.
18. Murray, 'Discerning the Dynamics of Doctrinal Development'.

in the context of this coherentist approach.[19] Although it is pragmatic coherence that is sought, it is typically an experience of *in*coherence which is initially significant, insofar as such incoherence can be associated with a particular doctrine, practice or systemic attitude. Murray gives the example from his own Roman Catholic Church of clerical and institutional abuse but other cases are easy to find; for example, interchurch families, experiences of women in the Church, and lack of empowerment for the laity. This also has significance for the starting point of Receptive Ecumenism, which is not passing over a draft article for colleagues to comment upon, but acknowledging real wounds and dysfunctions in one's own tradition and actively seeking healing from the other, even if this entails reweaving the web of existing beliefs, practices and structures.

This tripartite coherence may be the nearest we get to finding hard criteria for 'receiving with integrity' in Murray's work. However, outside of Murray's own writings, these underlying methodological commitments are rarely referenced in the literature or practice of Receptive Ecumenism. However, one scholar who has entered into conversation with Receptive Ecumenism in terms of foundational theology is Ormond Rush, in his work on the interpretative role of the sense of faith.[20] Can an examination of Rush's hermeneutical commitments act as a complementary resource, thickening Murray's description of the fundamental structure and dynamics of Receptive Ecumenism?

Rejuvenating Reception

Rush uses the notion of 'rejuvenating reception' to describe the dynamic and creative act of appropriation of tradition by individuals and communities.[21] In the literary aesthetics and hermeneutics

---

19. Paul D Murray, 'Searching the Living Truth of the Church in Practice: On the Transformative Task of Systematic Ecclesiology', in *Modern Theology*, 30/2 (2014): 251–81.

20. Ormond Rush, 'Receptive Ecumenism and Discerning the *Sensus Fidelium*: Expanding the Categories for a Catholic Reception of Revelation', in *Theological Studies*, 78/3 (2017): 559–572.

21. Ormond Rush, *The Reception of Doctrine: An Appropriation of Hans Robert Jauss' Reception Aesthetics and Literary Hermeneutics* (Rome: Gregorian University Press, 1997).

of Hans Robert Jauss,[22] this is applied to a work of art, but in Rush's appropriation of Jauss, it is the objects of God's revelation which are received, in various sites of reception (*loci receptionis*). Significantly, one of these sites of reception which Rush enumerates is to be found in ecumenical encounter and dialogue.[23] He argues that the 'creative, innovative, ecclesial activity' of rejuvenating reception, above all, 'has implications for processes of dialogue and the discovery of truth within the Church and between the churches today'.[24] I will focus on two of the numerous triads which Rush appropriates from Jauss: firstly, a 'triad of readings'; and secondly, a 'triad of senses'. Both of these are involved in the reception of a work.[25] Although the literature on Receptive Ecumenism makes little reference to reception hermeneutics,[26] I argue that key elements of Murray's proposal closely parallel these triads, in turn opening up the possibility of further insights from reception hermeneutics being applied in Receptive Ecumenism. Two main lines of convergence can be drawn: i) a structural resonance between the 'triad of readings' and Murray's programmatic outline of Receptive Ecumenism; and, ii) a parallel between the 'triad of senses' and the dynamics of receptive ecumenical learning.

The first triad describes the process of interpretation in terms of three successive 'readings': firstly, a pre-reflective aesthetic moment, reimagined by Rush as the sense of faith; secondly, a reconstructive hermeneutical activity which views the work critically and in historical context; thirdly, an applicative hermeneutics, through which answers for the present horizon and a rejuvenating reception of tradition are possible. If we look at the initial programmatic outline of Receptive Ecumenism, it shows a remarkable similarity to this triple

---

22. Hans Robert Jauss, *Aesthetic Experience and Literary Hermeneutics*, translated by Michael Shaw, (Minneapolis: University of Minnesota Press, 1982).

23. Four objects of reception are identified, which are received in twelve *loci receptionis*. The eleventh of these sites is 'reception between separated churches and ecclesial communities'. Rush, *Reception of Doctrine*, 189–211.

24. Rush, *Reception of Doctrine*, 185.

25. On the 'triad of senses' and 'triad of readings' from Jauss' hermeneutics see Rush, *Reception of Doctrine*, 225–34, 315–25.

26. It is given a passing mention in Riccardo Larini, 'Texts and Contexts—Hermeneutical Reflections on Receptive Ecumenism', in *Receptive Ecumenism and the Call to Catholic Learning*, edited by Paul D Murray (Oxford and New York: Oxford University Press, 2008), 89–101.

reading, with pre-reflective, critical and applicative moments. In the preface to the first Receptive Ecumenism volume, Murray describes the essence of the project as follows:

> [Receptive Ecumenism] might be best expressed in terms of: (1) the dreaming of dreams; (2) the testing of such dreams for their viability; and (3) the discerning together of what might either hinder or promote their embodied ecclesial realization. These are the three voices, the three concerns, in which and in accordance with which the volume unfolds. We might refer to them respectively as the poetic, the analytic, and the pragmatic or, alternatively, as the imaginative-constructive, the critical-constructive, and the practical-organizational. They might be held to be the three key voices in which all good ecclesial theology is performed.[27]

The resonance between these three voices and the three readings of reception hermeneutics is a promising sign in terms of thickening Murray's methodology as far a *structural* similarity goes. So too is Rush's argument that 'fuller understanding in the search for truth requires the readings of others'.[28] But what about the *dynamics* of performing interpretation in receptive mode? From Jauss' aesthetics, Rush has drawn attention to three senses involved in reception: *poiesis*, *aesthesis* and *catharsis*. Can these also be found in Receptive Ecumenism?

A starting point is Murray's description of Receptive Ecumenism as an act of 'ecclesial *poiesis*', constructive ecclesial theology 'poised between given circumstances and accumulated understanding, on the one hand, and necessary accountability, refinement, and anticipated actualization, on the other'.[29] So too for Rush, 'there is a creativity at the core of a believer's on-going act of faith which is a

---

27. Murray acknowledges the resonance of these three voices with John Henry Newman's reflections on the threefold office of the Church—priestly, prophetic, and kingly—and Nicholas Lash's subsequent use of these as 'three intertwined, all-pervasive aspects of authentic Christian living in relation to God.' Paul D Murray, 'Preface', in *Receptive Ecumenism and the Call to Catholic Learning*, edited by Paul D Murray (Oxford and New York: Oxford University Press, 2008), ix–xv, at xi.
28. Rush, *Reception of Doctrine*, 325.
29. Murray, 'Preface', xii.

reconstructive and reinterpretative imagining . . . It is here that the rejuvenating reception of doctrine begins.[30] *Poiesis* represents a creative, productive sense, allowing a dynamic of 'Christian newness' in the act of reception and enabling the production of a 'new work'.[31] In an ecumenical context, the new work might be a formal text such as *Baptism, Eucharist and Ministry*,[32] or key documents emerging from ARCIC—the kind of documents which Anton Houtepen sees as belonging to a 'future-oriented Christian tradition'[33]—but the broad reach of Receptive Ecumenism emphasises that we may also receive more informally, and more locally, from many aspects of another tradition—devotional, practical, doctrinal, or organisational. When the 'dreaming of dreams' is seen in this light, it is clear that such a starting point is not opposed to the disciplined theological work required for structural and sacramental unity, but rather the exercise of a particular hermeneutical sense which is essential in interpreting a tradition afresh. Through imaginative engagement, in faith, with the lived experience of the other, the creative activity of *poiesis* is allowed full play without prematurely applying analytical or pragmatic constraints. The language of 'ad-hoc strategy', and 'virtuous virus', and the non-linear reasoning Murray employs, does not indicate a lack of method; rather the creative employment of *poiesis* is a reconstructive, hermeneutical act.

What about the other two senses—*aesthesis* and *catharsis*? Are these also discernible in the literature and practice of Receptive Ecumenism? In Rush's hermeneutics, following Jauss, these terms have a subtly different meaning to their everyday sense. *Aesthesis* complements the productive imagination of *poiesis* with a receptive sense of recognition. It is concerned with identity in relation to a wider set of reference points in order to create a meaningful whole.[34] As Walter Kasper has noted, any possibility of creative appropriation

---

30. Rush, *Reception of Doctrine*, 218.
31. Rush, *Reception of Doctrine*, 73.
32. World Council of Churches, *Baptism, Eucharist, and Ministry* (Geneva: World Council of Churches, 1982).
33. Anton Houtepen, 'Hermeneutics and Ecumenism: The Art of Understanding a Communicative God', in *Interpreting Together: Essays in Hermeneutics*, edited by Peter Bouteneff and Dagmar Heller (Geneva, Switzerland: WCC Publications, 2001), 1–18.
34. Rush, *Reception of Doctrine*, 73–76, 229–32.

through reception requires creative *integration*,[35] and for Murray's post-foundationalist approach it is above all the metaphor of reweaving which encapsulates this striving for dynamic coherence. Similarly for Receptive Ecumenism, *aesthesis* involves reweaving—with integrity—the web of doctrinal and pastoral relationships between *and within* churches, and between the Church and the world.

The final element of Jauss' aesthetic triad is *catharsis*. Against any notion of 'art for art's sake', *catharsis* involves an ethical orientation in the production and reception of a work and as such may involve changes even to deeply held traditions, such as an established canon of works or interpretative methods. In Receptive Ecumenism, the sense of *catharsis* is made concrete in a *therapeutic* mode. In the recognition of wounds and dysfunctions, a distance is recognised between the Church as actually experienced and what it is called to be in the fullness of Christ. One of the ways in which Jauss considers *catharsis* is in terms of how a reader identifies with the hero in a story. Whilst some modes of identification stress the continuity between reader and hero through association, imitation and sympathy, others— catharsis and irony—require a distancing from the hero, undergoing trials and suffering in order to make judgments.[36] This can be seen in Receptive Ecumenism when the interpreter *imaginatively* creates distance in order to acknowledge, and critically examine, an ecclesial wound or a dysfunction, whilst still being able to remain a member of the Church and indeed with the intention of Catholics becoming more Catholic, Anglicans more Anglican, and so on.[37]

---

35. 'Reception does not mean an automatic, merely passive, acceptance, but a lively and creative evolution of appropriation and integration.' Walter Kasper, *That They May All Be One: The Call to Unity Today* (London : Continuum, 2005): 140.

36. Jauss, *Aesthetic Experience and Literary Hermeneutics*, 177–81. A danger which Jauss identifies is that an aesthetic experience may not result in transformation. This may also be applied with considerable force to the ways in which a Christian tradition identifies with an idealised image of Church: 'The process of identification with an ideal model which one wishes to become does not always attain a personal synthesis. It can also slip back into the fantasy the daydreamer has always entertained about himself.' He names the dangers as 'the shifts from upward-looking admiration to mere marvelling at the extraordinary, from free emulation to unfree imitation, from a compassion that will act to the sentimental enjoyment of pain.' These dangers not only apply to the kind of 'blueprint ecclesiology' which Receptive Ecumenism seeks to avoid, but could equally apply to the danger of 'receiving with integrity' from the other being replaced by mere admiration for them in their difference or sentimentally feeling the pain of separation.

37. Murray, *Establishing the Agenda*, 16.

Conclusion

In this essay, I have made a selective comparison of two key architectural elements of Receptive Ecumenism as found in the work of Paul Murray with two of the hermeneutical triads Ormond Rush has transposed into theological mode from HR Jauss. Murray's Rescherian criteria, and his coherence model, illustrate something of what it means for Receptive Ecumenism to be a 'total ethic as simple and all-pervasive as the gospel it represents'. In this sense, the self-critical, recursive, expansive attitude towards one's own tradition, tested in terms of internal, extensive and pragmatic coherence, is a kind of 'deep grammar' for Receptive Ecumenism, situated beneath the apparent simplicity of its espoused principles. Similarly, Rush's reception hermeneutics, even in this brief examination, indicates that there is far more to the act of 'reception' than a passive approval or rejection of an ecclesial text. Given the compatibility between Murray and Rush outlined in this essay, it is reasonable to suggest that Rush's insights have the potential to extend further the conceptual tools available for exploring the deep roots and diverse dynamics of Receptive Ecumenism, complementing Murray's pragmatism with the resources of reception hermeneutics. Conversely, Receptive Ecumenism provides a concrete instance of what the ecumenical site of reception, one of Rush's twelve *loci receptionis*, looks like when churches, communities and individuals approach it in a receptive and creative mode.

In a contemporary context where ecumenists bemoan the lack of ecclesial reception for agreed ecumenical statements on the one hand, and, on the other hand, where the range and reach of Receptive Ecumenism appear to be expanding, an understanding of what is involved in the activity of reception is essential. Herein lies the value of Rush's work, which he himself has successfully applied to challenges within the Roman Catholic church, such as the interpretation of the Second Vatican Council, and the nature of the sense of faith (*sensus fidei*). The need for such an understanding is, I propose, especially true for an ecumenical approach which dares to lay claim to the term 'receptive ecumenism'. The synergy I have outlined here illustrates that the structural and dynamic resonance between Murray's approach and Rush's hermeneutics offers a potentially rich field of exploration, which could not only thicken the understanding of Receptive Ecumenism, but also contribute to the emerging field of ecumenical hermeneutics.

Bibliography

Avis, Paul, 'Are We Receiving "Receptive Ecumenism"?', in *Ecclesiology*, 8/2 (2012): 223–34.

Houtepen, Anton, 'Hermeneutics and Ecumenism: The Art of Understanding a Communicative God', in *Interpreting Together: Essays in Hermeneutics*, edited by Peter Bouteneff and Dagmar Heller (Geneva, Switzerland: WCC Publications, 2001), 1–18.

Jauss, Hans Robert, *Aesthetic Experience and Literary Hermeneutics* (Minneapolis: University of Minnesota Press, 1982).

Kasper, Walter, *That They May All Be One: The Call to Unity Today* (London: Continuum, 2005).

Larini, Riccardo, 'Texts and Contexts—Hermeneutical Reflections on Receptive Ecumenism', in *Receptive Ecumenism and the Call to Catholic Learning: Exploring a Way for Contemporary Ecumenism*, edited by Paul D Murray (Oxford and New York: Oxford University Press, 2009), 89–101.

Murray, Paul D, *Reason, Truth, and Theology in Pragmatist Perspective* (Leuven: Peeters, 2004).

Murray, Paul D, 'Preface', in *Receptive Ecumenism and the Call to Catholic Learning: Exploring a Way for Contemporary Ecumenism*, edited by Paul D Murray (Oxford and New York: Oxford University Press, 2008): ix–xv.

Murray, Paul D, 'Receptive Ecumenism and Catholic Learning: Establishing the Agenda', in *Receptive Ecumenism and the Call to Catholic Learning: Exploring a Way for Contemporary Ecumenism*, edited by Paul D Murray (Oxford and New York: Oxford University Press, 2008), 5–25.

Murray, Paul D, 'Discerning the Dynamics of Doctrinal Development: A Post-Foundationalist Perspective', in *Faithful Reading: New Essays in Theology in Honour of Fergus Kerr, OP*, edited by Simon Oliver, Karen Kilby, and Thomas O'Loughlin (London: T&T Clark, 2012), 193–220.

Murray, Paul D, 'Searching the Living Truth of the Church in Practice: On the Transformative Task of Systematic Ecclesiology' in *Modern Theology*, 30/2 (2014): 251–81.

Murray, Paul D and Murray, Andrea L, 'The Roots, Range and Reach of Receptive Ecumenism', in *Unity in Process*, edited by Clive Barrett (London: Darton Longman & Todd, 2012), 79–94.

O'Gara, Margaret, 'Receiving Gifts in Ecumenical Dialogue', in *Receptive Ecumenism and the Call to Catholic Learning: Exploring a Way for Contemporary Ecumenism*, edited by Paul D Murray (Oxford and New York: Oxford University Press, 2008), 26–38.

Pizzey, Antonia, 'On the Maturation of Receptive Ecumenism: The Connection between Receptive Ecumenism and Spiritual Ecumenism' in *Pacifica: Australasian Theological Studies*, 28/2 (2015): 108–25.

Pope Francis, 'Celebration of Vespers on the Solemnity of the Conversion of Saint Paul the Apostle' (25 January 2017) at <w2.vatican.va/content/francesco/en/homilies/2017/documents/papa-francesco_20170125_vespri-conversione-san-paolo.html>. Accessed 6 May 2018.

Pope John Paul II, '*Ut Unum Sint*: Encyclical on Commitment to Ecumenism' (25 May 1995), at <w2.vatican.va/content/john-paul-ii/en/encyclicals/documents/hf_jp-ii_enc_25051995_ut-unumsint.html>. Accessed 6 May 2018.

Rescher, Nicholas, *A System of Pragmatic Idealism*, volume 1, *Human Knowledge in Idealistic Perspective* (Princeton: Princeton University Press, 1992).

Rescher, Nicholas, *A System of Pragmatic Idealism,* volume 2, *The Validity of Values* (Princeton: Princeton University Press, 1993).

Rescher, Nicholas, *A System of Pragmatic Idealism,* volume 3, *Metaphilosophical Inquiries* (Princeton: Princeton University Press, 1994).

Rorty, Richard, *Philosophy and the Mirror of Nature* (Princeton: Princeton University Press, 1979).

Rowlands, Tracey, 'Ecumenism—What Future?', at <www.catholicweekly.com.au/prof-tracey-rowlands-ordinariate-lecture-ecumenism-what-future/>.

Rush, Ormond, 'Receptive Ecumenism and Discerning the *Sensus Fidelium*: Expanding the Categories for a Catholic Reception of Revelation', in *Theological Studies,* 78/3 (2017): 559–72.

Rush, Ormond, *The Reception of Doctrine: An Appropriation of Hans Robert Jauss' Reception Aesthetics and Literary Hermeneutics* (Rome: Gregorian University Press, 1997).

Slipper, Callan, *Enriched by the Other: A Spiritual Guide to Receptive Ecumenism*, (Cambridge: Grove, 2016).

South Australian Council of Churches, *Healing Gifts for Wounded Hands*, at <http://www.sacc.asn.au/_data/Healing_Gifts_for_Wounded_Hands_May_2014.pdf>. Accessed 6 May 2018.

Welby, Justin, "'Ecumenical Spring': Archbishop Justin's speech at World Council of Churches 70th Anniversary', at <www.archbishopofcanterbury.org/speaking-and-writing/speeches/ecumenical-spring-archbishop-justins-speech-world-council-churches>. Accessed 6 May 2018.

World Council of Churches, *Baptism, Eucharist, and Ministry* (Geneva: World Council of Churches, 1982).

A Forum for Theology in the World Vol 5 No 2/2018

The Means is the End: The Spiritual Heart of Receptive Ecumenism

Callan Slipper

On the face of it, Receptive Ecumenism is little more than a version of the sharing of gifts, something that has been in the toolkit of ecumenical practice for decades. One example of this is Churches Together England's leaflet *Sharing our Spiritual Treasures*, which provides guidelines for a group to 'Share stories and experience, Appreciate our different traditions, Find nourishment for our faith, Seek God in all things'.[1] No doubt Receptive Ecumenism does indeed have this dimension. But the impact of Receptive Ecumenism shows it to be more. There is something essential about it as a way of sharing spiritual gifts that allows it to go beyond an ecumenism of appreciation, good as that may be. This methodology is a form of relational approach, practicable in the most unpromising or challenging circumstances, that opens up the possibility of new learnings that can have far-reaching effects.

This, I hope to show, is because Receptive Ecumenism, in fact, contains an implicit and necessary spiritual discipline that is far deeper than the excellent practice of receiving gifts from one another. It goes to the heart of the nature of God and to the nature of the Church as it participates in God's life and being. It does this because Receptive Ecumenism is, in fact, rooted in the cross, and this means specifically the historical event of Jesus' crucifixion, theologically (and that is most truly) understood.

---

1. Churches Together in England, *Sharing our Spiritual Treasures*, at <https://www.cte.org.uk/Groups/240589/Home/Resources/Local_Ecumenism/Resources_for_local/Sharing_our_Spiritual/Sharing_our_Spiritual.aspx>. Accessed 12 June 2018.

The fundamental patterns of Receptive Ecumenism and what Jesus did on the cross are, in certain key respects, the same. In Receptive Ecumenism a church approaches the other in order to learn, admitting its own weakness. The encounter with the other church is not to dominate and control, but to engage, employing a practical humility that, as it finds things in the other that are useful for healing or mending its own weakness, sets itself in this sense below the other. Furthermore, in learning about the other, the learning church emphasises the gifts and the goodness of the other: it thus serves the other that is looked upon and learned about, highlighting the other's identity. This demands real charity. Indeed, to understand the other properly a loving gaze is needed, for love alone is completely attentive to the other. Thus the learning church is not merely using the church it learns about; in its gaining from the other it proclaims the other's value and, perhaps or even most likely, it shows the other beauties about itself that it had not till then realised. What we have here, therefore, is a love on the part of the learning church that is humble and other-focused and that, as it loves, reveals and strengthens the identity of the other.

The pattern of cruciform love displayed by the dying Jesus also has these characteristics, although it cannot be reduced to them alone. Here God in human flesh becomes radically the servant of humanity and, through human beings, of the cosmos. The One who served all creation in creating it, who serves it constantly by preserving it, now serves it by redeeming it, and makes himself nothing in the process: 'he was despised, and we held him of no account' (Isa 53:3). Jesus shows all the weakness of love that is the result of caring for the other to the point of being ready to give one's life. In doing so he reveals core aspects of the identity of the beloved other: on the one hand, its sinfulness in needing such a redeemer and, on the other hand, each human being's infinite value, because if the infinite spends itself without reserve for something, then that thing is of equal worth to the infinite. Human beings are both sinners and infinitely valuable. Jesus on the cross is thus humble, other-focused, and revealing of the other's identity—which, because of his redemption, can now be seen in its beauty.

Cruciform love as lived by the dying Jesus is thus displayed in Receptive Ecumenism. In both the other is approached with love that makes itself little. Both reveal the truth of the other that is loved. Both serve the other, and both receive from the other, albeit in different ways—the one to learn, the other to save.

What this indicates, however, is more than the congruence of Receptive Ecumenism with what could be called Christianity's core definition of love. Cruciform love has eternal relevance because it is the revelation of how God loves; that is, Jesus on the cross not only enacts human redemption, and thereby the redemption of all created being, he also demonstrates God's way of loving. God always loves in this wild and unconstrained manner. God is unconditional love.

For the *how* of loving points to God's innermost nature, since God acts according to what God is. Being perfect and unconditional love, as Richard of St Victor argues, the one God is Trinity because the perfection of charity must have another to love, in a dynamic that can only come to its highest fulfilment if the two who love each other look beyond each other and love a third.[2] Drawing upon both Augustine of Hippo's notion of the Lover, Beloved and Love as ways of speaking about the three Persons of the one God,[3] and upon Anselm's definition of God as that than which no greater can be conceived,[4] this gives an insight into the rhythm of God's trinitarian life. In so doing it underlines the spiritual heart of Receptive Ecumenism; it enters the dynamic of God's love. For the dynamism of trinitarian love places the Persons in a particular relation of total gift to one another. Hence, for instance, the love by which the Father generates the Son, if the Son is to be co-equal with the Father, with the same being, means that the whole of the Father's being is passed on. It is a form of self-emptying that holds nothing back and that becomes the 'radical servant' of the other – just like the dying Jesus on the cross in his love for God and for humanity. Jesus too 'passes on', in the Spirit,[5] his divine being to human beings so that they may share it with him, becoming co-heirs with him, God's adopted children.

---

2. See Richard of St Victor, *De Trinitate*, in *Trinity and Creation: A Selection of Works of Hugh, Richard, and Adam of St Victor*, edited by B Taylor Coolman and DM Coulter (Brepols: Turnhout, Belgium, 2010), book 3, especially chapters 2, 18 and 19.
3. See Richard of St Victor, *De Trinitate*, book 9.
4. See Anselm of Canterbury, *Proslogion, Complete Philosophical and Theological Treatises of Anselm of Canterbury*, translated by Jasper Hopkins and Herbert Richardson (Minneapolis, MI: The Arthur J Banning Press, 2000), 93–5.
5. Jn 19:30 says: 'When Jesus had received the wine, he said, 'It is finished.' Then he bowed his head and gave up his spirit.' The term translated 'gave up' is '*paredōken*' which means to hand over.

This is a pattern of relationship that is replicated among all three Persons of the Trinity. As Chiara Lubich puts it:

> The Father, in fact, in begetting the Son out of love, 'loses' himself in him, lives in him; he seems thereby to make himself nothing, but precisely in this making himself nothing out of love he is; he is Father. The Son, as echo of the Father, returns to the Father out of love, he 'loses' himself in him, lives in him; it seems therefore that he too makes himself nothing out of love, but precisely like this he is; he is Son. Equally the Holy Spirit: in his being mutual love between Father and Son, their bond of unity, he 'loses' himself in them, he makes himself nothing, in a certain way out of love, but precisely like this he is; he is the Holy Spirit.[6]

In Receptive Ecumenism when one church places itself before the other in order to learn, the learning church is, or at least is called to be, caught up in the love that sets aside everything for the other, so that, in the integrity of its own life, it can receive the gifts of the other. It makes itself nothing, as it were, in having no prejudices, no judgments: a truly listening, comprehending and attentive stance. It is receiving as love. At the same time, the receiving church offers a gift, in the act of its reception, to the giving church. For the giving church is invited to enter the same trinitarian dynamic of radical servant-hood. It makes is itself nothing, as it were, in sharing its gifts. Thus the relationship of Receptive Ecumenism provides the opportunity for the ecclesial dialogue partners to be brought into the dynamic of trinitarian life. This implies that Receptive Ecumenism is an opportunity to share in the eschatological fulfilment already achieved by Jesus on the cross and, until the completion of all things, imperfectly realised in history. Receptive Ecumenism, when practised according to the full meaning of its theological depth, is an eschatological event.

A consequence of this eschatological dimension of the relationship established by Receptive Ecumenism is a curious effect ecclesiologically speaking. It means that even before issues of doctrine, ministry, sacraments, or authority have been resolved – that is, before Faith and Order questions are settled in such a way as to bring

---

6. In a comment to a text written by her on 24 July 1949. See Marisa Cerini, *God who is Love* (New City Press: New York, 1992), 51–2.

churches into full visible unity – a truly ecclesial reality comes into being. This not to pretend that divisive institutional problems have been overcome: far from it. Nor is it to say that such challenges do not need to be faced and worked through. But it is to point out that the core of what it means to be 'Church', namely fellowship with one another within the uncreated fellowship of the triune Godhead, is already achieved. No doubt this communion with one another could be achieved more fully and still more effectively if the institutional aspects were resolved, especially since doctrine, sacraments and church order have such a profound impact upon our spiritual life. But the fact remains that, in the goodness and the grace of God, it is possible to experience the life of unity—the life that Jesus prayed for on the eve of his death–even before all the means and supports of unity are in place. Receptive ecumenism is witness to that.

Almost at counterpoint to that unity is another curious result of the eschatological and ecclesiological dimension of Receptive Ecumenism. It is that the unity that is achieved, on the pattern of the Trinity, does not in any way destroy the distinctions between those who are united. In God, of course, both the unity and the distinctions are absolute. Among human beings, participating in the divine life, both unity and distinction are lived according to the possibilities of creaturely nature. Hence as one church learns from another, differences between them become more clear. One church has something to learn from another precisely because it is not like the other. What is valued is the distinctive quality of the other. Yet what is distinctive about the learning church is also enhanced, since what is learned is appropriated within its own integrity. In other words, while in one sense the learning process lessens the differences between churches, because in acquiring something new (or recovering something they already implicitly had, but had in some sense lost) the two churches become more similar to one another, in another sense that very learning process enhances the identities of each of the dialogue partners. For the giving church, this is because its characteristic is put into relief, and for the receiving church it is because what is learned inevitably takes on a different life within the setting of an alternative polity.[7]

7. An example of this can be seen, at the time of writing, in the relations between Methodists and Anglicans in Britain and Ireland. In acts that in many ways parallel what is proposed by Receptive Ecumenism, the two traditions are taking significant steps on the way to visible unity. Although by no means the

But what takes place, significantly, in any breaking through of the eschatological reality of the Church into the lived experience of the here and now, is a shift in the relationship between the dialogue partners. It marks a new stage in their relationship. What is more, it presages further developments, because with the deeper mutual understanding that emerges, further issues can be discussed and looked at in the light of a real growing unity. Indeed, since unity is sharing together in the divine life (see, for instance, John 17:21–26), the issues are now looked at with the aid of the wisdom that comes from God. It is an application of the profoundly mystical core of ecumenism, where participation together in the living unity of God ('one, as we are one', Jn 17:22) becomes the methodology for an ever deeper understanding.

Such a profoundly spiritual experience offers the possibility of many practical results. The eschatological future, then, further impinges upon and shapes the challenges of the present. Setting aside for the moment the various official dialogues between the churches, one scheme that illustrates what this could achieve can be seen in the Receptive Ecumenism project in the North East of England, launched in 2007.[8] Here a comparative study of the workings of six participating denominational groups in the region was undertaken: the United Reformed Church (Northern Synod), the Salvation Army (Northern Division), Roman Catholic Diocese of Hexham and Newcastle, the Northern Baptist Association, the Methodist Church of Great Britain (the Districts of Newcastle and Darlington), the Church of England (the Dioceses of Newcastle and Durham).

Three research teams were appointed. They were each made up of: 1) key local practitioners and church personnel; 2) specialists in the fields of finance, management, and organizational studies from Dur-

---

only key dimension of these steps, one essential aspect is the reception of the historic episcopate, adapted within the integrity of their own life and polity, by Methodists. In 2014 the Methodist Church in Ireland received the historic episcopate from the Anglican Church of Ireland. Similar plans, though with some important differences, are under discussion by the Church of England and the Methodist Church of Great Britain. The intention is that although the historic episcopate in Methodism will always be an apostolic ministry of unity, it will not be exercised in exactly the same manner as within Anglican churches.

8. *Receptive Ecumenism and the Local Church: A Comparative Research Project in the North East of England*, 2016, at <https://www.dur.ac.uk/resources/theology.religion/ReceptiveEcumenismandtheLocalChurchFinalFullReport.pdf>. Accessed 25 June 2018.

ham University's Business School; and 3) theologians and sociologists or anthropologists of religion from each of Durham University's Department of Theology and Religion, local theological colleges, and the North of England Institute for Christian Education. There were, as they put it, 'three key trajectories of research',[9] each with its own research team. Some of the breadths of practical possibilities for Receptive Ecumenism can be seen in the areas the teams looked at, namely: *Governance and Finance* (focusing upon the organisational cultures and systems of authority, accountability, strategic planning, and finance, operative in each tradition); *Leadership and Ministry* (focusing upon how practices of leadership are seen and used within each of these traditions); and *Learning and Formation* (focusing upon how the respective cultures and identities of the churches are nurtured, transmitted, and shaped through the habits, practices, processes, and programmes implemented at various levels).

The project produced six reports, replete with practical suggestions to deepen reciprocal learning among the traditions by proposals enabling each tradition to live its vocation and mission more fruitfully, by providing a framework with which to understand the various traditions and encourage their effective work together, and by seeking to demonstrate a model of good practices whose way of living the ecumenical challenge in today's world could 'be offered to the wider church, both nationally and internationally.'[10] This illustrates something of the potential of Receptive Ecumenism, but it also serves to highlight the need for taking the eschatological dimension seriously. For none of these possible learnings will transform the churches or the relationships among them if the practical proposals do not bed down in real, personal and collective—and hence spiritual— praxis. A better-organised system of consultation, for instance, only serves the life of the church and the relationship among Christians if it is carried out in the same spirit of generous learning and humble love that characterises the eschatologically-based discipline of Receptive Ecumenism.

It should be clear, therefore, that Receptive Ecumenism to achieve its end demands practical discipline by all who participate in it, a spirituality capable of living up to the challenges of learning and, above all, of loving. There is no way that the action of grace at work in the

---

9. *Receptive Ecumenism and the Local Church,* 7.
10. *Receptive Ecumenism and the Local Church,* 10.

Christian life can produce the fruits of the Spirit without the transformation of the individual believer; in like fashion, there is no way that the same Spirit at work in those engaged in Receptive Ecumenism can open the dialogue partners to the fullness of learning that takes place within their sharing together in the trinitarian life unless they allow the Spirit to mould their characters, behaviour and actions.

But the good news is that this transformation is, so to speak, the stock-in-trade of the Christian life. It comes by no means as simply a matter of chance, without a definite act of faith in response to God. Yet once entered into within the context of Receptive Ecumenism, another joyful discovery lies before the Christian. The act of loving in order to learn already sets up the communion that is sought with the other. Which is to say that if traditions come together under the yoke of the spiritual discipline of cruciform love, and seek to learn from one another, the relationship they achieve now is already a foretaste of the relationship they seek to achieve in the end. It is the essence, indeed the living reality—experienced in the present—of the final unity. Receptive Ecumenism is thus more than a modest but useful strategy for carrying on the conversation when dialogue is difficult. It is a possibility of experiencing the ultimate unity even before that unity is fully reached. The final end is effective in the present means.

Bibliography

Anselm of Canterbury, *Proslogion, Complete Philosophical and Theological Treatises of Anselm of Canterbury*, translated by Jasper Hopkins and Herbert Richardson (Minneapolis, MI: The Arthur J Banning Press, 2000).

Cerini, Marisa, *God who is Love* (New City Press: New York, 1992).

Churches Together in England, *Sharing our Spiritual Treasures*, at <https://www.cte.org.uk/Groups/240589/Home/Resources/Local_Ecumenism/Resources_for_local/Sharing_our_Spiritual/Sharing_our_Spiritual.aspx>. Accessed 12 June 2018.

Multiple authors, *Receptive Ecumenism and the Local Church: A Comparative Research Project in the North East of England*, 2016, at <https://www.dur.ac.uk/resources/theology.religion/ReceptiveEcumenismandtheLocalChurchFinalFullReport.pdf>. Accessed 25 June 2018.

Richard of St Victor, *De Trinitate* in *Trinity and Creation: A Selection of Works of Hugh, Richard, and Adam of St Victor*, edited by B Taylor Coolman and DM Coulter (Brepols: Turnhout, Belgium, 2010).

Afterword
Receiving of Christ in the Spirit: The Pneumatic-Christic Depths of Receptive Ecumenism

Paul D Murray

I started out in the Foreword to this volume by saying that Geraldine Hawkes' 'Meditation on the Water of Life', Vicky Balabanski's pair of biblical reflections on Colossians 3 and Romans 8, and Antonia Pizzey's and Callan Slipper's respective contributions, each in differing yet complementary ways serve to take us deeply into the spirit and soul of Receptive Ecumenism. Focussing specifically, for the moment, on the passages chosen by Vicky Balabanski, Colossians 3 and Romans 8, and reflecting the inextricable interrelatedness of pneumatology and Christology, we might usefully think here in terms of the 'Christo-pneumato-centric' or, perhaps better, 'pneumato-Christo-centric' character of these passages. Such a perspective has strong resonance both for me personally and for the deep story and instincts of Receptive Ecumenism; particularly so when taken in conjunction with the thematically related passages in Ephesians and the prologue to the fourth gospel.[1]

As I explore elsewhere, some of the consequent implications of this perspective are: that each of us individually, and each of the Christian traditions collectively, is called to a unique participation in God's love, God's Spirit, made visible for us in Christ; and, with this, that each is in turn also called to be a unique enacting and showing of this love in Christ. The understanding at work here is that the Spirit-

---

1. For some reflection on all of this and its ecclesiological relevance, see Paul D Murray, 'Living Catholicity Differently: On Growing into the Plenitudinous Plurality of Catholic Communion in God', in *Envisioning Futures for the Catholic Church*. Cultural Heritage and Contemporary Change Series VIII, Christian Philosophical Studies 23, edited by Staf Hellemans and Peter Jonkers (Washington, DC: Council for Research in Values and Philosophy, 2018), 109–58.

risen, Spirit-energised, Spirit-ascended, Spirit-transfigured cosmic Christ really *is* the 'all and in all' (Col 3:11), in whom each—in his/her/their uniqueness—is destined to shine in glorious particularity, for all eternity, in the gathered communion of saints in Christ and the Spirit (compare 2 Cor 4:6).

The language of destiny is important here. Whilst, in the circumstances of this order, the realisation of this vision might currently seem counterfactual, when viewed in the bigger perspective of our faith-assured destiny, it is not in doubt, whether at the individual level or at the collective ecclesial level. When viewed in this perspective, these passages do not function first and foremost as coded ethical imperatives, encouraging us to strive anxiously for an ideal but elusive potential victory which, together with God, we might just possibly be able to achieve if all should work out well. No, the primary function of these passages is to disclose and assure us of our already-foreseen and already God-given eschatological destiny. As such, our appropriate response is one of hope-filled, patient conformity, and Spirit-drawn participation; not one of assertive, anxious-striving: glory be to God whose power, working in us in the Spirit-filled Christ and the Christ-shaped Spirit, can do and is doing infinitely more than we can ever ask or imagine (compare Eph 3:20).

It is important to keep this cosmic, contemplative context and orientation of Receptive Ecumenism clearly in view. With this, and following from it, it is equally important to recognise that whilst Receptive Ecumenism points us to things of absolute, eschatological significance—our fulfilled communion in Christ and the Spirit—it does not do so either as a form of idealised moral injunction, detached from the reality of things, or as a form of avoidance and second-best compensation for the seemingly endlessly deferred character of eschatological realisation. On the contrary, Receptive Ecumenism seeks *both* to attend closely to this fundamental, eschatological, God-given reality of things *and* to ask what it means, in quite specific terms, to live in anticipatory accordance with this fundamental reality in the nitty-gritty particularities, messiness, and felt challenges of the actual experienced reality of our ecclesial lives and communities. Moreover, Receptive Ecumenism seeks to do this in ways which at once serve, *as primary focus*, our respective greater flourishing *within* our own respective traditions and, *as secondary consequent focus*, a greater flourishing and depth of communion *between* our traditions.

It is in this manner that Receptive Ecumenism is to be properly understood as both: 1) a way of deeper Spirit-drawn growth into the fullness of Christ within a particular tradition; and, related to this, 2) a means of serving and leading us further toward the abiding ecumenical goal of full structural and sacramental communion in appropriate diversity. It is, perhaps, significant that this particular way of walking the ecumenical journey has come into sharper focus precisely during a period of ecumenical disillusioning, in which prospective achievement of full structural and sacramental communion has very definitely come to be seen as lying beyond the capacities of mere human striving and foreseeable, programmable planning.[2] This is a way which can only be walked through active dependency; through a constant *leaning-in* to the Spirit of transforming love; and as a hope-filled anticipation of our fulfilled communion in Christ and the Spirit.

Complementing this, in my Foreword to this volume and from my perspective as a systematic theologian, I also place due emphasis—amongst other things—on the proper role of formal theological analysis, reconceiving, scrutiny, and testing as an essential moment in this way of Receptive Ecumenism.[3] At this point, however, and in

---

2. See The Third Anglican—Roman Catholic International Commission, *Walking Together on the Way: Learning to Be the Church—Local, Regional, Universal* (Erfurt 2017), which explicitly adopts Receptive Ecumenism as its shaping method and does so precisely in the context of acknowledging the significantly changed context in which formal bilateral Anglican–Catholic dialogue now operates, see particularly 'Preface' (iv) and §§5, 10, 15, 17–19, 21, 78–9 (2–3, 4, 5, 6, 7, 22), available at: http://www.vatican.va/roman_curia/pontifical_councils/chrstuni/angl-comm-docs/rc_pc_chrstuni_doc_20180521_walking-together-ontheway_en.pdf.

3. To clarify, ARCIC III's *Walking Together on the Way* identifies: a) a range of felt difficulties within the respective Anglican and Catholic traditions; together with, b) various ways in which each tradition might potentially pursue receptive learning from the other tradition in relation to these felt difficulties. The document does not, however, itself pursue the detailed, critical-constructive analysis, reconceiving, and testing that is required for the process of Receptive Ecumenism to be pursued in full. Such work is beyond the scope, mandate, and time-capacity of the Commission and constitutes, rather, a key aspect of its subsequent reception; particularly so its scholarly-theological reception but also its wider reception within the *sensus fidelium* and its subsequent formal ecclesial reception. To put this in the terms I alluded to in the Foreword, *Walking Together on the Way* "attends seriously to what is", to the point of beginning "to

light of the very definitely practical orientation of a number of the contributions to this volume, let me again emphasise that, vitally important though it be, such theological analysis is by no means *all*. On the contrary, it is a *moment*—perhaps of some duration—in broader processes of life. As such and as was also noted in the Foreword, this necessary analytical theological moment is situated within and properly comes second to the needs and desires, the wounds and the wants, of the fractured, frail, ecclesial body of Christ. Theological testing and analysis are to these ecclesial needs and desires as mind is to the heart: an essential resource but as servant, not master; any other understanding of this relationship is an idolatrous and distorting misperception of the proper role and end of theology.

This in turn opens up the question as to the identity of Receptive Ecumenism: is it defined and closed? Something which only ever manifests in one way? Or is it more open than that? Something which manifests differently in diverse circumstances, as the various contributions to this volume might appear to suggest? Well, one of the images I use for Receptive Ecumenism is of it being more like an adaptive 'virtuous virus' than it being an identikit franchise that must be reproduced in identical form in all circumstances. As such, the identity and character of Receptive Ecumenism is clearly relatively open.

Equally, however, whilst Receptive Ecumenism may intentionally be *under*-defined, it is *not* completely *un*defined. It cannot rightly just become anything to anyone without thereby ceasing to be characteristically Receptive Ecumenism and being reduced to nothing more than a fresh conceptual label for whatever someone was already ecumenically inclined to do. Despite the deliberate openness of interpretation and application, there nevertheless are some identifiable Receptive Ecumenical family characteristics which, in one way or another, must always be seen to be in play—albeit in varying ways in various different circumstances—if a particular initiative is to be

---

imagine what might be", but without fully testing these imaginings in a way that can yet support actual practical change. As such, *Walking Together on the Way* is both explicitly shaped throughout by the principles of Receptive Ecumenism and serves to bring us to the threshold of where the specific systematic task of critical-constructive analysis, reconceiving, and testing needs to begin. It provides an agenda for systematic ecclesiology to pursue.

properly regarded as a Receptive Ecumenical endeavour.[4] One such defining character trait is the aforementioned recognition of the need for a balancing of heart and mind: for the necessary situating of critical-constructive theological analysis in the context of the suffering and desiring ecclesial body of Christ.

Lest, however, this should be further misinterpreted, it is equally important to state that this characteristic emphasis on the necessary role of critical-constructive theological analysis, imagining, and testing in the overall Receptive Ecumenical endeavour does *not* mean that only professional theologians can be appropriately involved in the process. Quite the contrary is in fact the case. Indeed, Receptive Ecumenical thinking does not even presuppose that all participants in the relevant learning processes are actively committed ecumenists for whom ecumenical engagement and vocation have traditionally been a key part of their Christian life. All it presupposes is that participants are concerned for the health of their own challenged and conflicted ecclesial contexts and are prepared to attend seriously to whatever relevant learning can be had from other contexts.

In this regard, I often cite the example of parochial parish councils in the Catholic context, which are permitted but not required by Catholic canon law. Consequently, even where they exist, they can be of varying functionality and practical significance relative to real decision-making. Unsurprisingly, then, it is not an uncommon phenomenon for priests and people alike to become frustrated with the lived reality of their parish council and to want to renew and refresh it in some way. To aid this they might just conceivably—but likely not—go to ask the advice of a neighbouring parish which is known to have a well-functioning parish council; or they might, more likely, arrange for a consultation and formation programme through the diocesan adult education and pastoral formation team. What, however, they would most likely not think to do would be to invite members of the local Anglican parish, Methodist circuit, United Reformed congregation, or Baptist church to come and talk about how issues of parochial/congregational decision-making are typically handled in their own respective ecclesial contexts, and with what supporting

---

4. See Paul D Murray and Andrea L Murray, 'The Roots, Range, and Reach of Receptive Ecumenism', in *Unity in Process: Reflections on Ecumenism*, edited by Clive Barrett (London: Darton Longman & Todd, 2012), 79–94, particularly 86–9.

structures, processes, habits, and cultural norms/ethos in play. Such an exercise in real Receptive Ecumenism could have an immensely important contribution to make to expanding the default Catholic imagination concerning what is desirable and possible in the Catholic context. Moreover, we can safely assume that the majority of the members of a typical Catholic parish council, who would quite likely gain great benefit and interest from such a receptive learning process, would not consider themselves to be committed ecumenists. They would just be an average range of parishioners with various specific ecclesial/missional interests and forms of expertise to offer, who are each concerned for the health of their parochial community life and witness.

Now, of course, there needs to be discernment, scrutiny, and prudence exercised in such a process as this. Not all that might appear attractive in another ecclesial context will be currently conceivable in the Catholic context relative to existing authoritative norms which lie outside of the parochial sphere to alter. And, indeed, not all that *is* so conceivable will actually be practical in a given context. Equally, however, not all that priests and/or people might immediately assume to be either currently inconceivable or just impractical will in fact be so when properly scrutinised. It is here that the specific contribution of the professional theologian can usefully be made—either directly, through personal involvement, or mediated by relevant resources— serving the analysis and potential re-weaving of the web of Catholic tradition with dynamic integrity.

More generally, if we adopt the receptive ecumenical orientation in relation to felt difficulties in our church life, then points will naturally arise, at every level of church life and in every context, where questions concerning the ability of one ecclesial community to learn from another ecclesial community, with appropriate integrity intact, will come to the fore. This is the proper place of formal theological analysis in the Receptive Ecumenical process: in-situ and in conversation with the ordinary conversations of the church.[5] Nor, of course, does this negate the very considerable amount of 'back-room' work

---

5. Of relevance to this understanding of the engaged role of formal theological analysis—for which read "systematic theology"—situated between the ordinary conversations of the church and the analytical expertise of the academy, see Nicholas M Healy, 'What is Systematic Theology?', in *International Journal of Systematic Theology*, 11 (2009): 24–39, particularly 38.

which theologians will likely need to pursue in order to be able to speak into such situations with sensitivity, imagination, and integrity; as too, it need not negate the capacity of theologians to be anticipating questions and issues, and so readying themselves to be able to make appropriate and effective contribution, when timely.

For those seeking further reassurance—beyond ARCIC III's *Walking Together on the Way*—that the claimed priority of the practical and the claimed focus on lived ecclesial realities does in fact find real space in the literature and formal projects in Receptive Ecumenism, one might well look to the multi-year North East of England Comparative Research Project in Receptive Ecumenism and the Local Church.[6] Here three teams of theologians, social scientists, educators, management experts, church officials, and ecumenical officers pursued a series of studies into the empirical realities of the churches of the North East of England, the felt difficulties arising there, and the opportunities for potential learning across the churches in relation to such difficulties. Again, one might turn to the invaluable resource booklet produced by Callan Slipper, *Enriched by the Other: A Spiritual Guide to Receptive Ecumenism*,[7] and the related Churches Together in England on-line course, *Embracing the Other: A Resource for Receptive Ecumenism*;[8] as too the excellent booklet produced by Geraldine Hawkes through the South Australian Council of Churches, *Healing Gifts for Wounded Hands: The Promise and Potential of Receptive Ecumenism*.[9]

But what about those projects and initiatives which understand themselves to be sailing under the Receptive Ecumenical flag but wherein the kind of mutual receptivity which is in view is at the entirely informal, relational, and practical levels of, for example, shared witness, shared mission, and mutual openness? Such initiatives are capable of issuing in all kinds of informal, interpersonal, and practical learning but without there ever being any formal theological

---

6. See https://www.dur.ac.uk/theology.religion/ccs/projects/receptiveecumenism/projects/localchurch/.

7. Callan Slipper, *Enriched by the Other: A Spiritual Guide to Receptive Ecumenism* (Cambridge: Grove Books, 2017).

8. See https://www.cte.org.uk/Groups/306183/Home/Resources/Theology/Receptive_Ecumenism/Resources/Embracing_the_Other.aspx.

9. See http://www.sacc.asn.au/_data/Healing_Gifts_for_Wounded_Hands_May_2014.pdf.

dimension. As earlier noted, there can sometimes be a tendency to name just anything Receptive Ecumenism and to assume it is really nothing more than a new way of speaking about anything at all ecumenical, other than it helpfully emphasising the need for us to be open to and valuing of each other. Well, viewed in one way, there is clearly some basic affinity and resonance between such projects and the ethos and values which are at work in Receptive Ecumenism. However, given what has been said repeatedly, both here and in the Foreword, about the essential role of critical-constructive theological analysis and reconceptualising in Receptive Ecumenism—in service of the potential reweaving of the webs of respective traditions with dynamic integrity—it is important to recognise that there is a key sense in which Receptive Ecumenism cannot just be all things to all people. To put this in terms of traditional ecumenical categories, Receptive Ecumenism is properly to be understood as an instrument of Faith and Order ecumenism and not simply as another name for all that might sail under Life and Work ecumenism.[10]

Equally, however, if some of the entirely practical projects which lay claim to the title of Receptive Ecumenism are not in fact examples of Receptive Ecumenism in any full-blooded theological sense, it is nevertheless important to recognise that it is precisely such initiatives which can perform the invaluable service of thawing, tilling, watering, and seeding previously frozen ground, and so making it ready to open up to the larger, more directly theological questions and matters which are in play in Receptive Ecumenism proper. It is a performative contradiction and practical nonsense when we make false oppositions of different approaches to the ecumenical task—as has too often happened—rather than seeking for a sense of complementarity in difference. There are multiple strands to the ecumenical cord: that is what gives it its strength; or, to alter the image, multiple notes in the ecumenical chord, which lend it depth and resonance. The fact that Receptive Ecumenism is playing, with some freshness, upon certain of these notes and drawing out certain of these strands, and doing so in a manner well-fitted for our ecumenical times, does not thereby make the other ecumenical notes and cords irrelevant.

---

10. See Paul D. Murray, 'In Search of a Way', in *The Oxford Companion to Ecumenism*, *edited by* Geoffrey Wainwright and Paul McPartlan (Oxford: Oxford University Press, 2017), available at: http://www.oxfordhandbooks.com/view/10.1093/oxfordhb/9780199600847.001.0001/oxfordhb-9780199600847-e-45.

Shifting tack somewhat, the centrality of pneumatology to Receptive Ecumenism has already been noted and reflected upon in a preliminary manner in the Foreword. It is, however, worth teasing this out a little further, particularly so as regards the assumed inextricable interrelationship of pneumatology and Christology, Spirit and Word.[11] Lying behind the dynamic view of Christian tradition which Receptive Ecumenism assumes[12] is the conviction that the Spirit is not adequately understood simply as the communicating 'third' in God, who only ever follows on and flows from a mediating 'second'. Rather, the Spirit is here understood as the personal acting of God; the loving energy that is God's life in action; the initiating-transforming agency of God, who from all eternity is searching out the inexhaustible hidden depths of God (compare 1 Cor 2:10) and bringing them to ever fresh expression in the Word/Son. In this way of thinking, the pneumatic and the Christic are always intertwined, co-existent, and coincident: where the Spirit can well be understood as the initiating-transforming acting and disclosing of God, the Word is the expressed form of this acting and disclosing, the performed act shown forth, the spoken Word expressed. Again, where the Spirit can well be understood as bringing the Word to voice and action, the Word can well be understood as giving form and expression to the Spirit's movement.

Thinking in this way of the Spirit as the initiating-transforming, personal loving agency of God helpfully reminds us that there is proper dynamism rather than stasis in the life of God. Talk of God as the 'unmoved mover' and of the 'eternal now' of divine life can potentially mislead us here. But the "unmoved mover" idea need not imply that God is neither constantly moving created things nor in movement within God's own life: in fact, quite to the contrary. It simply and properly maintains that there is nothing which moves God

---

11. Here a key text is Yves MJ Congar, *The Word and the Spirit*, translated by David Smith (London / San Francisco: Geoffrey Chapman / Harper & Row, 1986 [1984]). It needs be acknowledged, however, that the understanding of the Holy Spirit traced here goes some way beyond Congar's own suggestive lines of thought in thinking of the Spirit as having an initiating-transforming agency in the Godhead and not simply in the economy.

12. See Paul D Murray, 'Discerning the Dynamics of Doctrinal Development in Postfoundationalist Perspective', in *Faithful Reading: Essays in Honour of Fergus Kerr*, edited by Simon Oliver, Karen Kilby & Thomas O'Loughlin (London & New York: T&T Clark, 2012), 193–220.

from 'without'; that there is no external compulsion requiring or constraining God's own utterly free movement. Similarly, the idea of the 'eternal now' is not about absence, emptiness, and stasis but about absolute fulfilment and utter actualisation such that there is and can be no unrealised potential whatsoever in God, the potential realisation of which is left in any doubt. As such, the 'eternal now' is the utterly fulfilled moment of God's one total being-in-act of love, in which every possible movement of love is fully actualised all at once. Properly understood, this is the perfection of action not its absence.

It is also—linking with what I was reflecting on earlier about our destiny in Christ and the Spirit not being in fundamental doubt—the grounds for the fact that we can utterly depend on God, for there is nothing about the being-in-act of God's fully actualised love which is in any way in doubt, or for which any kind of striving is required. Indeed, we can deepen this point further by directly linking this understanding of God as the absolutely fulfilled act of perfect love—the 'eternal now'—with the notion of God as the utterly free 'unmoved mover'. By doing so, we can come to a helpful appreciation of the proper significance of the non-necessity of creation to God, which does not mean that God is distant and uncaring in relation to creation. On the contrary, it means that creation is not brought into being on account of any need on God's behalf, which it is then the task of creation to satisfy, but purely and simply as an unnecessary, entirely gratuitous—albeit fitting—overflow of God's goodness and love, with the intention of bringing something other than God into being in order to share in God's life not for God's sake but for its own sake.[13] As such, given that creation in its entirety and in its myriad particularity is in no way instrumental to God's being and life but a gratuitous act of non-manipulative love, we can absolutely trust, whatever appearances to the contrary might suggest, that we are held in and destined for love without limit. We can lean-in to that, and find ourselves held in it and moved by it, and so able to live out of it.

But what does this all mean when we shift from the perspective of the perfected act of the 'eternal now' to the conditions of finitude, temporality, and dimmed, partial knowledge in which we are currently required to live (compare 1 Cor 13:12) and here grow into our

---

13. See Rowan Williams, 'On Being Creatures', in Williams, *On Christian Theology* (Oxford and Malden, MA: Blackwell, 2000), 63–78.

eternal destiny? Well, to the extent that Einstein's famous $E = mc^2$ might enable us to think of matter as cooled-down and configured energy, then perhaps we might analogously think of time as slowed down eternity: as what happens when the 'eternal now' is transposed into the conditions of finitude. Whatever might be the case with the perfected total act of God's love, for us there is sequence, discrete action, even effort as we journey into God, who is our beginning, our end, and our constant sustaining life.

However, viewed and lived contemplatively, with a due sense of pneumatic-Christic depth, we should not let the temporal conditions of finitude, and the need for act and some exertion which these necessarily entail, devolve into anxious striving and constant, harried activity. Thinking specifically in relation to the ecumenical context, for example, we do not need to attempt to achieve everything at once. We should do what is possible and what is necessary, here and now, and what is within our actual sphere of influence, in the belief that today's visible and realisable steps will open tomorrow's as yet unforeseeable possibilities. We can trust that the ecumenical endeavour and journey has a future—and Receptive Ecumenism a key role to play in that—because we each have a future which is held in the assurance of the eternal presence and utterly dependable, absolutely fulfilled being-in-act of God's love.

This orientation towards the anticipatory living of our future destiny in the conditions of the present might well in turn lead us to ask what form of unity Receptive Ecumenism is taking us towards? Well, given what was earlier noted about each of us individually and each of the Christian traditions collectively being an absolutely unique sharing in and showing of God's love in Christ and the Spirit, with each having an irreplaceably important contribution to make to the prospective gathering of all in the 'all and in all' of Christ and the Spirit, we can be sure that the promised unity of our ecumenical future will not be any bland grey uniformity. Nor will it equate with the reductionism of post-denominationalism, which tends, in practice, not so much towards sustaining and enriching the diverse particularity of the traditions but towards a wide familial commonality of each being various versions of charismatic evangelicalism and pentecostalism. By contrast, the form of unity—better, communion—at issue and anticipated in Receptive Ecumenism is one which takes the abiding significance of particularity and diversity absolutely seriously.

In this regard, it is important for us to get right what kind of ethic of receptive hospitality and self-effacing humility is properly assumed in and encouraged by Receptive Ecumenism as getting this wrong can lead to diminishment rather than enrichment. The fact that Receptive Ecumenism believes that we should not and must not push our own particular gifts on others does *not* mean that we should in any way diminish or deny these gifts. Nor does it mean that we should cease to work out of them. On the contrary, Receptive Ecumenism values deep inhabitation of traditions. It is what enables us to be confident performers of and witnesses to our respective traditions in ways that in turn enable others to learn from us, as their needs and contexts might suggest. Indeed, we need to be sufficiently confident in our giftedness—understood precisely as God-given gifts rather than as self-achievement—as to be capable also of humbly recognising both our own performative limitations and difficulties and the differing giftedness of others, from which we can usefully learn and receive in ways that will deepen, expand, and enrich our respective ecclesial identities.

In the latter part of his own contribution to this volume, Callan Slipper also helpfully recognises that Receptive Ecumenism is most fundamentally about this kind of deepening, enriching, and expanding of ecclesial traditions—through learning and receiving from each other's gifts in relation to our own tradition's respective difficulties—in a way that requires no loss of anything authentic. This point is deserving of further emphasis: any relinquishing, or loss, in the context of Receptive Ecumenism should be a relinquishing of what is false, or unnecessarily narrow, or distorted, rather than a loss of anything positive and authentic. We do not cease being who we are. Rather, the vision is that we will be freed to become more fully and more fluently who we most deeply already are and are called to be; that each of our traditions will be able to grow, each in its own way and by following its own path, to a place of recognition of ourselves in the other, of the other in ourselves, and of each being held together in Christ and the Spirit.

Inspired by the ancient hymn in Philippian 2, it has become commonplace in much contemporary theology and spirituality to adopt kenotic language of 'self-emptying' as a means of seeking to speak of something like the kind of dynamic I have just traced.[14] Indeed Callan Slipper himself plays with this imagery in the earlier part of his contribution. Along with others, I think we need to exercise some caution here. Kenotic imagery can very easily give rise to some significant confusions and distortions, and lead us in a quite different direction to that which I traced earlier. Quite apart from the destructive pathologies of Christian spirituality and holiness which can result from the prioritising of self-diminishment, theologically it is just very odd to think in any substantive terms of a divine self-*emptying*: God's loving self-giving in Christ and the Spirit is not in any sense the emptying, or diminishing, of God's being-in-act but its fullness.

By contrast, and as means of seeking to preserve what I think is right in this kenotic instinct whilst protecting against these difficulties, I prefer to think in terms of there being a fundamental divine movement of 'life-giving, self-giving', which is always from fullness to fullness, without diminishment, and which is always creative-transformative. This movement of life-giving, self-giving can well be thought of as the movement of love which is the Spirit; it is this same movement which we see performed throughout the life of Jesus—most specifically in his life unto death on the cross—with the necessarily creative-transforming dimension of this divine life-giving, self-giving being manifest both in the effects on those whom he encountered during his earthly lifetime and, most definitively, in his being raised in the power of the Spirit and all that flowed from that. In turn, the movement in Receptive Ecumenism which, recognising one's own tradition's difficulties and felt-need for others' gifts, responds to the opening of space for loving transformation can well be understood as a graced, created sharing in this pneumatic-Christic life-giving, self-giving of God.

So, returning to the question as to the particular form of ecclesial unity which Receptive Ecumenism anticipates and seeks to serve: borrowing from our sisters and brothers in the LGBT+ community, we might well say that what we have in view is a rainbow unity, a rainbow communion, the gathering of all in full ecclesial communion

---

14. See, for example, John A Jillions, 'Kenotic Ecumenism', in *The Oxford Companion to Ecumenism, edited by* Geoffrey Wainwright and Paul McPartlan (Oxford: Oxford University Press, 2017), available at: http://www.oxfordhandbooks.com/view/10.1093/oxfordhb/9780199600847.001.0001/oxfordhb-9780199600847-e-46.

across and through significant diversity.[15] Indeed, rainbow is too limited an image, for it is, by analogy, not just the visible spectrum but every possible frequency on the ecclesial electromagnetic spectrum that is to be brought into configured communion in Christ and the Spirit.

Or again, my favourite image for the future reconciled church is that of a fully-decked family Christmas tree: not one with the uniformity of colour and style that one finds in shopping arcades but one with the kind of non-uniform, organic assemblage of diverse particular items, variously gathered on trips, collected, and passed on through generations, each treasured in its uniqueness, and then brought into concert with each other in the dressing of the tree. I love to look at our decked tree from various different angles and perspectives, letting my eyes go slightly out of focus in order to enjoy its shimmering unity, before then bringing them back into focus and appreciating each ornament in its particularity of relation with the others.

Receptive Ecumenism does not simply hold out hope for the future achievement of the fully-decked ecclesial tree with all its diverse shimmering particularity in orchestrated harmony. Rather, Receptive Ecumenism seeks to provide a way in which we can live now, oriented in anticipation on that hope, and in ways which will take us substantively closer to its realisation. This is a way of leaning-in to and living out of the Spirit so that the full ecclesial presence of Christ might be more clearly manifest for the salvation of the world.

---

15. Compare:
No one has monopolies on truth.
Rather, like a prism's dispersed side
Rainbowed truth allows us variants
Of another side's pure gathered light.
Micheal O'Siadhail, '3. Steering. Canto 5. *A Beckoned Dream* (iii)', *The Five Quintets* (Wako, TX: Baylor University Press, 2018), 229–33, here at 231.

List of Contributors

Vicky Balabanski is Senior Lecturer in New Testament at Flinders University, South Australia, and Director of Biblical Studies at the Adelaide College of Divinity and the Uniting College of Leadership and Theology. She has lived and worked in various parts of Europe and the Middle East, including a year in Jerusalem as a post-doctoral fellow at the Hebrew University. She is on the board of the Centre for Ecumenical Studies in Australia, and her publications in this field include 'The Prayer of Jesus as an inspiration and call to ecumenical unity: looking for "Jesuanic resonance" in John 17:20–21', in *Jesus–Gestalt und Gestaltungen. Rezeption des Galiläers in Wissenschaft, Kirche und Gesellschaft*, Festschrift für Gerd Theissen, edited by P von Gemünden, M Küchler, D Horrell (Göttingen: Vandenhoeck & Ruprecht, 2013), 635–650.

Geraldine Hawkes is the Ecumenical Facilitator with the South Australian Council of Churches and Executive Secretary for Leaders of Christian Churches South Australia. She has extensive experience across various Church settings in Australia and beyond, especially in the areas of Archdiocesan Governance, Pastoral Care, Spirituality, Ecumenism, Ethics, Women's experience of Church and Interfaith Relations. Contributions to the Receptive Ecumenism movement include the handbook 'Healing Gifts for Wounded Hands: *the promise and potential of Receptive Ecumenism*', and other resources, available at www.sacc.asn.au .

Paul D Murray a married lay Catholic, is Professor of Systematic Theology at Durham University, where he is also Dean-Director of the Centre for Catholic Studies. He has served on the Editorial Board of *Concilium International*; is a former President of the Catholic Theological Association of Great Britain; and a member of the third phase of work of the Anglican-Roman Catholic International Commission (ARCIC III). He has also served as a Consultor to the Pontifical Council for Justice and Peace. His publications include *Reason, Truth and Theology in Pragmatist Perspective* (2004), *Receptive Ecumenism and the Call to Catholic Learning: Exploring a Way for Contemporary Ecumenism*, editor, 2008, and *Ressourcement: A Movement for Renewal in Twentieth Century Catholic Theology*, co-editor with Gabriel Flynn, 2012. He has also contributed many essays to leading journals and scholarly collections. His current monograph project is entitled *Catholicism Transfigured: Conceiving Change in the Church.*

Denis Edwards is a professorial fellow in theology at Australian Catholic University, Adelaide campus and a member of ACU's Institute for Religion and Critical Inquiry. He is a priest of the Catholic Archdiocese of Adelaide, a Fellow of the International Society for Science and Religion and a member of the International Methodist-Roman Catholic Commission. Recent publications include *Christian Understandings of Creation: The Historical Trajectory.* (Minneapolis MN: Fortress Press, 2017); *The Natural World and God: Theological Explorations* (Adelaide, SA: ATF Theology, 2017) and *Partaking of God: Trinity, Evolution and Ecology* (Collegeville, Minnesota: Liturgical Press, 2014).

Karen Petersen Finch is Associate Professor of Theology at Whitworth University. She is also a Minister of Word and Sacrament in the Presbyterian Church (USA). She is a Fellow of the Lonergan Institute of Boston College. Karen looks at ecumenical dialogue through the lens of Bernard Lonergan's theological method, particularly dialogue between Roman Catholic theology and her own Calvinist/Reformed tradition. 'Contemplating a Roman Catholic Reception of the Heidelberg Catechism', in *Worship, Tradition, and Engagement: Essays in Honor of Timothy George* (Eugene, Oregon: Pickwick Publications, 2018), and 'The Reformed Rejection of Natural Theology: Dialectic and Foundations', in *METHOD: Journal of Lonergan Studies*, 6/2 (2015): 19–34.

Elizabeth Welch is a Minister in the United Reformed Church UK, serving in Hackney, London; former Moderator of the General Assembly of the URC; Chair of Society for Ecumenical Studies, UK; Co-chair of International Reformed Anglican Dialogue; she has spoken on local ecumenism at conferences in Canada, Germany, South Africa and Australia and has written various articles on ecumenism. Elizabeth Welch and Flora Winfield *Travelling Together: A Handbook on Local Ecumenical Partnerships* (London, Churches Together in England, 1995 and 2004).

Antonia Pizzey is a lecturer in systematic theology at the School of Theology at Australian Catholic University. Her publications on Receptive Ecumenism include her article: 'On the Maturation of Receptive Ecumenism: The Connection between Receptive Ecumenism and Spiritual Ecumenism', in *Pacifica*, 28/2 (2015): 108–125. She was part of the Global Ecumenical Theological Institute of the World Council of Churches in 2013, and contributed a chapter to the volume which came out of that experience: 'God is Love: Ecumenism of the Heart', in *Prospects and Challenges for the Ecumenical Movement in the 21st Century*, edited by David Field and Jutta Koslowski (Geneva: Globesethics.net Global, 2013).

Doru Costache is Senior Lecturer in Patristic Studies at St Cyril's Coptic Orthodox Theological College, a member institution of the Sydney College of Divinity, and Honorary Associate of Department of Studies in Religion at the University of Sydney. He is co-author of *Dreams, Virtue and Divine Knowledge in Early Christian Egypt* (Cambridge University Press, forthcoming) and co-editor of *Well-Being, Personal Wholeness and the Social Fabric* (Cambridge Scholars Publishing, 2017).

John Littleton is a retired Anglican minister in the Diocese of Adelaide. He has forty-six years' experience as an Anglican priest serving three parishes and ministering as a Consultant in Education in four Australian Anglican Dioceses. John is a member of the Anglican Ecumenical Network (AEN) in the Diocese of Adelaide. He is a member (Anglican appointee) of the South Australian Council of Churches (SACC), Community for Ecumenical Learning and SACC President (October 2017–October 2018): http://www.tjhlittleton.com.au

Sara Gehlin is a post-doctoral researcher at the University of Helsinki in Finland. Her doctoral dissertation concerns the issue of just peace in contemporary ecumenical theology. Her recent publications in English include the journal article 'Unity, Action, and Spirituality. Prospects and Challenges at the Intersection between Contemporary Receptive Ecumenism and Nathan Söderblom's Ecumenical Vision', in *One in Christ*, 52/1 2018, and the report *Educating for Peace. A Theological Task in Contemporary Times*, The Expert Group for Aid Studies, Stockholm 2017.

Gabrielle R Thomas is a Post-doctoral Research Associate at Durham University and a Minor Canon at Durham Cathedral, UK. Her current research explores ecclesial learning about women's experience of working in UK churches through Receptive Ecumenism. She researches and teaches Ecumenism, Historical Theology and Theological Anthropology. Her publications include *The Image of God in the Theology of Gregory of Nazianzus* (Cambridge: Cambridge University Press, 2019) and 'A Call for Hospitality: Learning from a Particular Example of Women's Grass Roots Practice of Receptive Ecumenism in the U.K', in *Exchange*, 47/4 (2018): 335–350.

Gregory A Ryan is Adult Formation Advisor for the Catholic Diocese of Hallam, England. He is currently completing doctoral studies on theological hermeneutics and Receptive Ecumenism at Durham University.

Callan Slipper is the Church of England's National Ecumenical Officer and the author of *Five Steps to Living Christian Unity* (New City Press: New York, 2013) and *Enriched by the Other: A Spiritual Guide to Receptive Ecumenism* (Grove Books: Cambridge, 2016)

Lightning Source UK Ltd.
Milton Keynes UK
UKHW010700290121
377856UK00002B/132